MW01598529

How Can the Obesity Epidemic Be Controlled?

Jill Karson

San Diego, CA

About the Author
Jill Karson is an editor and author of nonfiction books. She
lives in San Diego with her husband and three children.

For more information, contact:
ReferencePoint Press, Inc.
PO Box 27779
San Diego, CA 92198
www.ReferencePointPress.com

Picture Credits:

Cover: Shutterstock.com/Umit erdem
 6: Depositphotos
 9: Depositphotos
13: Depositphotos
16: Monica Schroeder/Science Photo Library
21: Thinkstock Images
26: Depositphotos
29: Thinkstock Images
34: © Samantha Appleton/White House/Corbis

37: Thinkstock Images
42: Michael A. Jones/Zuma Press/
    Newscom
47: Depositphotos
51: Associated Press
55: Depositphotos
59: Richard B. Levine/Newscom
65: Matthew McDermott/Newscom
67: Depositphotos

LIBRARY OF CONGRESS CATALOGING-IN-PUBLICATION DATA

Names: Karson, Jill, author.
Title: How can the obesity epidemic be controlled? / by Jill Karson.
Description: San Diego, CA : ReferencePoint Press, Inc., 2017. | Series:
  Issues in society | Audience: Grade 9 to 12. | Includes bibliographical
  references and index.
Identifiers: LCCN 2016011927 (print) | LCCN 2016015861 (ebook) | ISBN
  9781682820742 (hardback) | ISBN 9781682820759 (eBook)
Subjects: LCSH: Obesity--Prevention--United States--Juvenile literature. |
  Physical fitness--Health aspects--Juvenile literature. |
  Lifestyles--Health aspects--United States--Juvenile literature.
Classification: LCC RC628 .K346 2017 (print) | LCC RC628 (ebook) | DDC
  362.1963/9800973--dc23
LC record available at https://lccn.loc.gov/2016011927

CONTENTS

A Global Phenomenon

At the turn of the century, the World Health Organization (WHO) classified obesity as a growing epidemic. More than a decade and a half later, obesity has become a truly global phenomenon. Today, despite palpable efforts to contain rising weights, more than 2 billion people—nearly one-third of the world's population—are overweight or obese, and that number is rising. The number of individuals classified as overweight or obese in the United States is particularly high. Data released by the Centers for Disease Control and Prevention (CDC) indicate that fully 69 percent of US adults fall into this category.

A Burden on Public Health

Obesity has been called one of the most serious public health challenges of the twenty-first century for good reason. It affects young and old, male and female, and all races and ethnicities. It has few geographical boundaries. Perhaps most alarming, America—and the world—now faces a wave of obesity-related chronic diseases that threaten personal well-being and overburden health care systems. Because childhood obesity has reached epidemic proportions, these debilitating lifestyle diseases are increasingly diagnosed in children and teenagers.

Public health officials have identified many factors that have played a role in the current epidemic. On a personal level, poor diet and lack of physical activity are seen as the likely culprits of weight gain. Efforts that focus on giving individuals the skills to maintain healthy weights have long been part of the national discourse about obesity. This concept of individual responsibility has given rise to a $61 billion-dollar-a-year weight-loss industry, which includes books, diet and exercise programs, medications, specialty foods, and even bariatric surgery, a procedure that surgically shrinks the stomach and prevents overeating.

Many Are Unable to Keep Weight Off

Despite the public consciousness about how to lose weight, for most people, weight-reduction diets prove futile. While many people initially lose weight, the real problem, for most, is keeping the weight off. Harriet Brown is the author of *Body of Truth: How Science, History, and Culture Drive Our Obsession with Weight—and What We Can Do About It.* According to Brown, with weight-loss diets "you'll likely lose weight in the short term, but your chance of keeping it off for five years or more is about the same as your chance of surviving metastatic lung cancer: 5 percent. . . . In reality, 97 percent of dieters regain everything they lost and then some within three years."[1] Research even shows that of the 179,000 bariatric surgeries performed in 2013, as many as 50 percent of patients will regain some or all of the weight lost.

Many doctors and other health advocates agree that sustained weight loss—or preventing weight gain in the first place—is so difficult because today's food industry has created an environment that leads to overeating. The last few decades have seen the explosive growth of highly caloric, cheap, processed foods—sugary breakfast cereals, frozen pizzas, burgers, fries, sugary sodas, and an endless variety of snack foods and other convenience foods. The inescapable presence of all this junk food, as well as supersized portions, sophisticated marketing campaigns, fewer home-cooked meals, increasing soda sizes, and more sedentary lifestyles are among the many factors that have brought the nation to its current dilemma.

> "In reality, 97 percent of dieters regain everything they lost and then some within three years."[1]
>
> —Harriet Brown, author of *Body of Truth: How Science, History, and Culture Drive Our Obsession with Weight—and What We Can Do About It.*

Just as there is no single cause of obesity, there is no magic cure that will bring the current epidemic to a standstill. A 2014 report by the Robert Wood Johnson Foundation and the Trust for America's Health reported that despite interventions to address obesity, little progress has been made. These failures are not unique to the United States. Commenting on the seemingly intractable nature of the problem, Christopher J.L. Murray, director of the Institute for Health Metrics and Evaluation, says that "in the last three decades, not one country has achieved success in reducing obesity rates."[2] The Obesity Prevention Source at the Harvard T.H. Chan School of Public Health touches on why

Nearly one-third of the world's population is either overweight or obese, making obesity one of the most serious public health challenges of the twenty-first century.

obesity is such a challenge: "The fact that the obesity epidemic didn't flash over countries like a wildfire—rather it smoldered and then slowly grew year after year—has made it even more difficult to combat, since its causes have become so intertwined into the social, environmental, and governmental fabric."[3]

Efforts to Control Obesity

Health experts hope that efforts to combat obesity will gain traction as many levels of society come together to dismantle the barriers to living a healthy life. At the government level, a number of regulations have been put forth to create an environment that promotes normal weights. Some of the solutions proposed include taxes on sugary drinks, more stringent regulations on junk food advertising, and zoning laws that discourage the establishment of junk food outlets near schools and other areas where children congregate. Other initiatives support the development of walking and biking paths and other community spaces that encourage physical activity. As the nation wrestles with the problem of obesity, these and other interventions will be tested in the public arena.

1 What Are the Facts?

The WHO defines *obesity* as "an abnormal or excessive fat accumulation that may impair health."[4] The body mass index (BMI) is a scale that relates body weight to height and is used to classify obesity in adults; it is calculated by dividing a person's weight in kilograms by the square of his or her height in meters. A high BMI indicates weight that is higher than what is considered healthy for a given height. The WHO, the CDC, and other health organizations define *obesity* as a BMI greater than 30; *extreme obesity* is defined as a BMI greater than 40. Children are more difficult to measure using BMI calculations because height, weight, age, and gender need to be considered.

The prevalence of obesity has skyrocketed in recent decades. In the United States, the CDC reports that obesity rates have doubled since 1960; today over one-third of the adult population is obese. This equates to approximately 78.6 million obese adults. The WHO projects that obesity rates could be as high as 50 percent in the United States by the year 2025.

Some groups are more affected by obesity than others. Among racial and ethnic groups, Native Americans and Alaskan natives have the highest rates of adult obesity, with 54 percent considered obese. This is followed by African American adults, with over 47 percent classified as obese; Hispanics, with over 42 percent obese; and whites, with over 32 percent obese.

Obesity Rates Are Rising Among Young People

What's more, obesity is reaching earlier and earlier into the lives of America's youth. In 2001, 6 million young people in America were overweight or obese. Today approximately 12.7 million, or 16.9 percent, of children and adolescents aged two through nineteen years are considered obese. The distribution of obesity in this age bracket in regard to race and ethnicity shows similar trends to those seen in adults: in 2011 through 2012, over 22 percent of Hispanic children and adolescents were classified as obese, compared to over 20 percent of African American youth and just over 20 percent of non-Hispanic whites. The Obesity Action Coalition reports that these obese children are 70 percent more likely to be obese in adulthood.

Obesity is spreading to every corner of the globe. A study funded by the Bill and Melinda Gates Foundation examined obesity data from 188 countries. In all, the prevalence of overweight or obese people in the world increased from 857 million in 1980 to 2.1 billion in 2013. The study found that the developing world has been hit particularly hard by rising obesity rates. Although obesity was once restricted to industrialized societies, over 60 percent of today's obese people live in developing countries.

The study also found that obesity is concentrated in certain regions. Of the 671 million obese individuals in the world, over 50 percent live in just ten countries—the United States, China, India, Brazil, Mexico, Russia, Egypt, Germany, Indonesia, and Pakistan. In 2013, when the data was analyzed, the United States accounted for the highest proportion of obese individuals anywhere on the planet, with 13 percent of the world's total. Moreover, the worldwide spread of obesity shows no signs of stopping. In light of these alarming trends, the WHO and other public health organizations have declared obesity a global epidemic.

> "If there ever was a multifactorial condition, obesity is it—a complex of interacting genetic, metabolic, behavioral, hormonal, psychological, cultural, environmental, and socioeconomic factors."[5]
>
> —University of California, Berkeley, School of Public Health.

A Multifaceted Problem

Obesity and weight problems are caused by many factors. At a basic level, obesity results from excess calorie consumption and insufficient physical activity. However, experts at the School of Public Health at the University of California, Berkeley (UCB), say this equation does not tell the complete story:

> People gain weight when there's an energy imbalance—they consume more calories than they burn. But it's overly

simplistic to blame the obesity epidemic solely on people eating too much because of lack of willpower and on sedentary lifestyles. If there ever was a multifactorial condition, obesity is it—a complex of interacting genetic, metabolic, behavioral, hormonal, psychological, cultural, environmental, and socioeconomic factors, some of which are easier to alter than others.[5]

Some groups are more affected by obesity than others. Among racial and ethnic groups, Native Americans and Alaskan natives have the highest rates of obesity, followed by African Americans, Hispanics, and whites.

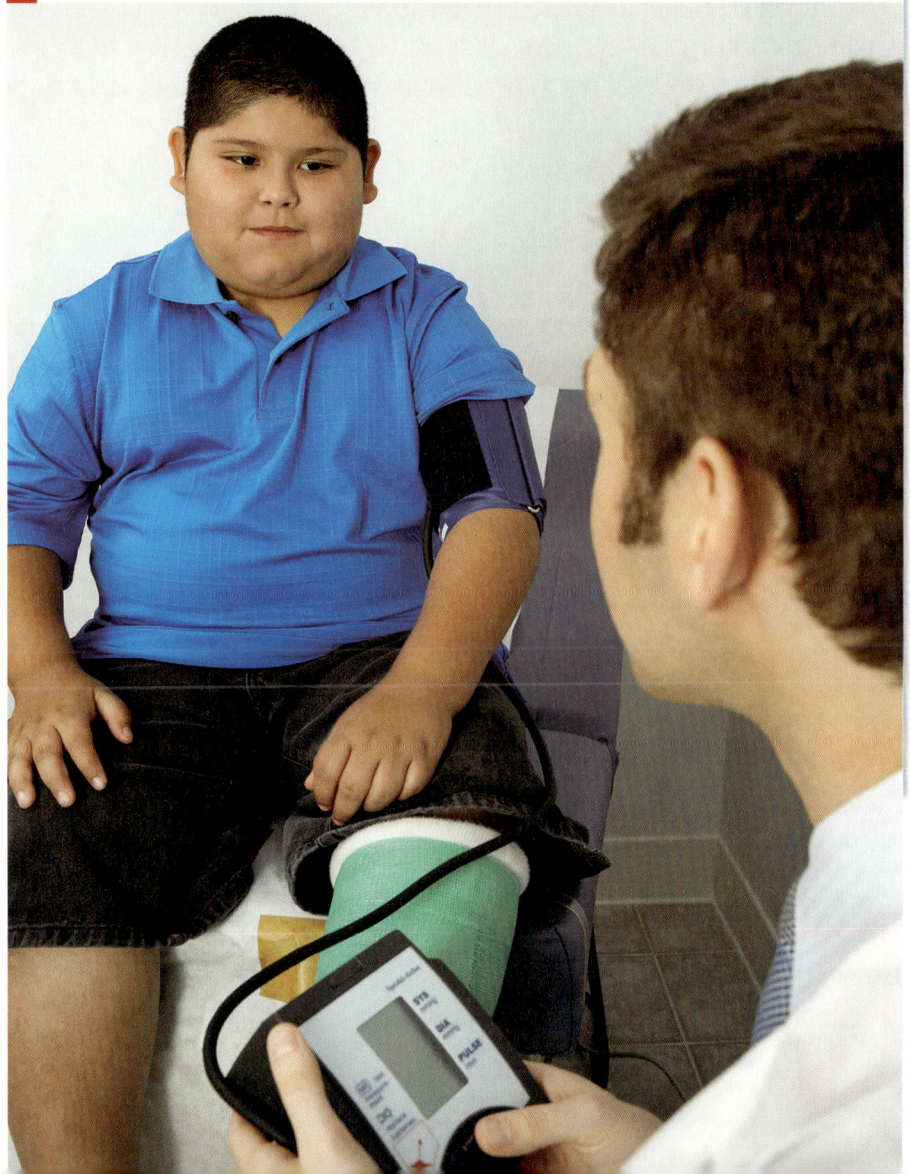

Most public health officials recognize that today's food environment has changed dramatically in the last three decades; certain government programs have likely played a role in these changes. For example, the US Farm Bill, which pays hundreds of millions of dollars each year to farmers across the country, may have contributed, in part, to the widespread proliferation of cheap, calorie-dense fast foods and processed foods served in huge portions. This program was developed to subsidize corn, wheat, and other storable grains to support farmers in tough times and to provide Americans with an affordable, reliable supply of food that would not spoil. Today these cheap, subsidized crops are used to manufacture the prime ingredients in processed foods, such as high-fructose corn syrup, cornstarch, vegetable oils, and other mainstays of the junk food industry. Highly processed junk food, as a result, is affordable and ubiquitous. A study from the University of North Carolina reports that Americans get 60 percent of their daily calories from processed foods, including soda, sugary cereals, cookies, chips, and other highly caloric, nutritionally empty foods.

Data on dietary intake in the United States confirm that Americans are taking in more calories than ever. According to the US Department of Agriculture (USDA), American adults have increased their daily calorie intake by as much as 530 calories a day over the last three decades. Over the course of a year, this increase can add up to fifty-three pounds (24 kg) of fat. At the same time that average daily calorie consumption has increased, studies consistently indicate that Americans have become much less physically active. This is partly due to the explosion of technological advances—computers and televisions, for example—that lead to more sedentary lifestyles that may promote weight gain. While solutions to the unfolding epidemic remain elusive, the hazards of all this extra weight have long been known. Obesity increases the risk of many chronic diseases and disorders, saps worker productivity, and overburdens health care systems.

Health Risks

Being overweight or obese is associated with a number of serious health risks. In 2013 the American Medical Association officially

The Relationship Between Poverty and Obesity Is Changing

The Food Research & Action Center (FRAC) is a nonprofit organization dedicated to improving childhood nutrition. Here, FRAC describes the complicated relationship between poverty and obesity.

> While all segments of the U.S. population are affected by obesity, one of the common myths that exists is that all or virtually all low-income people are far more likely to be obese. In this generalization, two facts commonly are overlooked: (1) the relationship between income and weight can vary by gender, race-ethnicity, or age and (2) disparities by income seem to be weakening with time.
>
> Recent research [shows] the complicated relationship between obesity and poverty. Overall, the research for a greater risk of obesity is more consistent for women and children (especially White women and children) of low-income or low-SES [socioeconomic status] than for men. In addition, there is evidence that where there are gaps between high- and low-income groups, they have been closing with time as those with higher incomes become more obese.

Food Research & Action Center, "Relationship Between Poverty and Obesity," 2015. http://frac.org.

recognized obesity as a chronic disease—that is, a long-lasting condition that can be managed but not cured. Obesity increases the likelihood of developing other chronic disorders, including heart disease; diabetes; hypertension, or high blood pressure; and stroke. According to the National Cancer Institute, obesity even raises the risk for certain cancers, including colon, postmenopausal breast, kidney, endometrial, and esophageal. Other research links obesity to liver, gallbladder, pancreatic, and other cancers. In fact, the American Cancer Society estimates that obesity is associated with nearly a third of all cancer deaths in the United States.

Even more concerning, many of these diseases and disorders are now being diagnosed in children. As more young people become obese, for example, pediatric heart disease is becoming more common. Type 2 diabetes is also on the rise; this is a disorder in which the body becomes resistant to the hormone insulin, causing high blood sugar. If untreated, diabetes can lead to kidney failure, heart disease, blindness, and circulatory problems that can lead to stroke. Heart disease kills nearly half of all people with diabetes. This dangerous disease used to be diagnosed primarily in middle-aged, overweight adults, but today teenagers represent a full third of all new cases.

A 2005 study in the *New England Journal of Medicine* reported that American children today will be the first generation in two centuries to live sicker and die younger than their parents. Robert H. Lustig is a pediatric endocrinologist and an expert on childhood obesity. He directs the Weight Assessment for Teen and Child Health Program at the University of California, San Francisco, Benioff Children's Hospital, and is a member of the Obesity Task Force of the Endocrine Society. Lustig describes the far-reaching health effects of childhood obesity:

> We're in the quiet before the storm. It's like what happens if suddenly a massive number of young children started chain smoking. At first you wouldn't see much public health impact. But years later it would translate into emphysema, heart disease, and cancer. . . . There is an unprecedented increase in prevalence of obesity at younger and younger ages without much obvious public health impact. But when they start developing heart attack, stroke, kidney failures, amputations, blindness, and ultimately death at younger ages, then that could be a huge effect on life expectancy.[6]

It is not just children who will suffer lowered life spans. According to the CDC, chronic diseases like diabetes and heart disease are now the leading cause of death and disability in the United States. They are the most common—and preventable—of all health problems. Although tobacco use and the overconsumption of alcohol contribute to these health conditions, many experts place the blame for the proliferation of chronic diseases squarely on poor diet and weight gain.

In the United States, highly processed junk food is affordable and abundant. On average Americans get 60 percent of their daily calories from processed foods, including soda, sugary cereals, cookies, chips, and other nutritionally empty foods.

A growing number of public health officials believe that obesity's contribution to chronic disease and premature death has been equal to, or even greater than, that of smoking. In fact, in 2001 the US surgeon general released a report that speculated that obesity and obesity-related diseases might soon overtake smoking as the leading cause of preventable death. Today the CDC reports that annual death rates associated with obesity are only slightly behind those of smoking, with 324,000 annual premature deaths for obesity and 443,000 for smoking.

The Stigma of Obesity

Deborah A. Cohen is a natural scientist at the RAND Corporation and the author of *A Big Fat Crisis: The Hidden Forces Behind the Obesity Epidemic— and How We Can End It.* According to Cohen, many people view overweight people as lacking self-control.

> The perceived link between lack of self-discipline and obesity has become so strong that overweight or obese people are often judged as less competent than their thinner peers. US Surgeon General Regina Benjamin was initially criticized for being overweight. What credibility would a health expert have if she couldn't practice a healthy lifestyle? When New Jersey Governor Chris Christie first began exploring a run for the presidency, his ample girth led many to question his fitness for office. To defuse the charge, he joked about his size by eating a doughnut on the *Late Show with David Letterman.* However, more recently, he admitted to getting LapBand surgery to help control his weight.

Deborah A. Cohen, *A Big Fat Crisis: The Hidden Forces Behind the Obesity Epidemic—and How We Can End It.* New York: Nation, 2014, p. 14.

Beyond the serious health risks associated with being overweight, the emotional toll of obesity can be great. Overweight and obese individuals often suffer from discrimination, social stigmatization, and poor self-esteem. Overweight children may be victims of bullying. Jamie Lee Peterson is a research associate at Yale University. She is part of a research team at the Rudd Center for Food Policy & Obesity at the University of Connecticut that examines weight bias and weight-related victimization. According to Peterson,

> Body weight is now one of the most common reasons youth are bullied; however, victimization of overweight youth continues to be overlooked in media, research and policy discussions. According to a recent survey, 41 percent of high school students perceived body weight as

the primary reason for teasing and bullying (followed by 38 percent for sexual orientation). In fact, more than three quarters of the students surveyed reported seeing overweight students being made fun of, called names, teased in a mean way, or teased during physical activity at school.[7]

An obese woman named Christine recalls her descent into depression when she started gaining weight during her teen years:

> Over the years, I have been insulted, verbally abused, even bullied, because of my weight. I have been treated as though I am invisible, worthless, and stupid—a pariah. As a result, I have felt invisible, worthless, and stupid, even though I know I am none of those things. The descent into depression began in my late teen years, which was the time when I started gaining excess weight.[8]

Or, as another woman remembers, "Nothing else mattered: that I was an A student; that I was kind and compassionate; that I had friends. These facts had no bearing. All that counted was the number on the scale."[9]

The Costs to Society

In addition to the negative effects on health and psychological well-being, obesity has substantial economic consequences; these include the direct costs associated with medical expenditures to treat obesity-related health conditions, such as physician visits, prescription drugs, and hospital care, and indirect costs, many of which are associated with lost economic productivity. The global price tag to manage the direct and indirect costs stemming from obesity is staggering: a report by the McKinsey Global Institute puts the global cost of obesity at $2 trillion annually. This means that obesity has nearly

> "Body weight is now one of the most common reasons youth are bullied."[7]
>
> —Jamie Lee Peterson, research associate at the Rudd Center for Food Policy & Obesity.

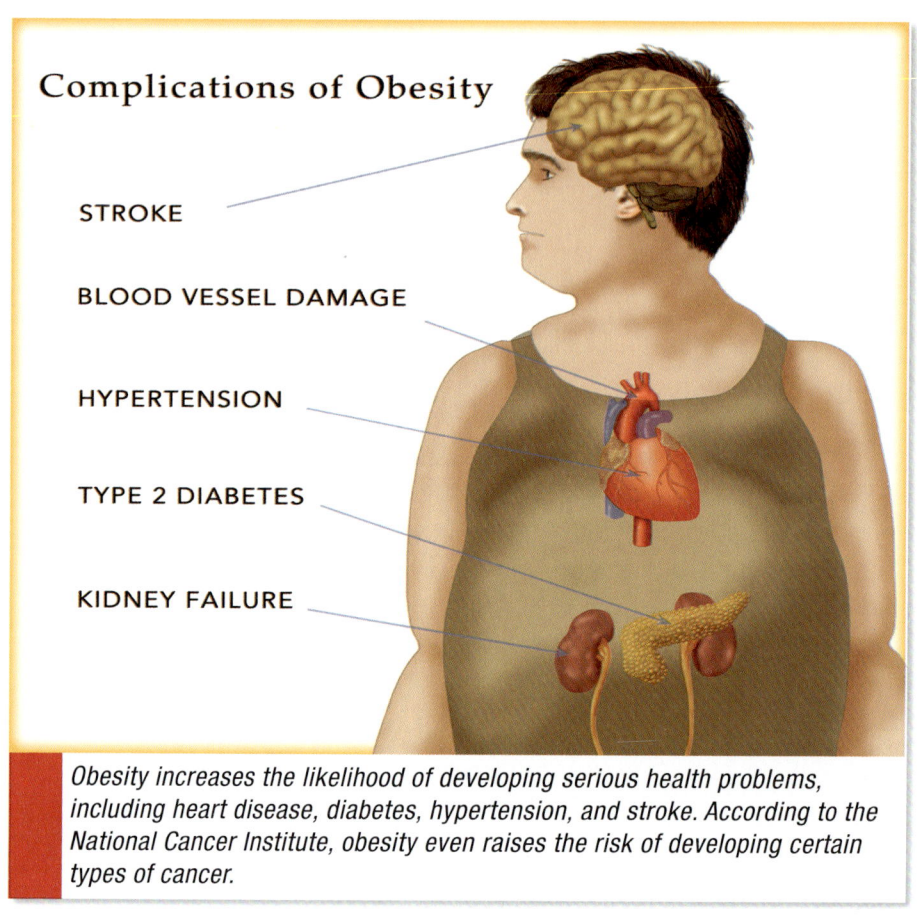

Complications of Obesity

STROKE

BLOOD VESSEL DAMAGE

HYPERTENSION

TYPE 2 DIABETES

KIDNEY FAILURE

Obesity increases the likelihood of developing serious health problems, including heart disease, diabetes, hypertension, and stroke. According to the National Cancer Institute, obesity even raises the risk of developing certain types of cancer.

the same economic impact as smoking, which has a global cost of $2.1 trillion annually. Costs attributable to obesity are also equivalent to the global cost of armed conflict, including war and terrorism, which costs over $2 trillion annually. Treating diseases related to obesity, such as heart disease, certain cancers, and diabetes, adds a major burden to most health care systems. In the United States, obesity-related medical expenditures are estimated at roughly $150 billion a year, up from $147 billion in 2008, as reported by the CDC; some estimates project that by 2018 the United States will be spending as much as $344 billion each year to treat obesity-related disorders.

A high percentage of these health care costs are used to treat heart disease, cancers, and high blood pressure. Diabetes is another expensive medical condition. The prevalence of this dangerous disease has risen dramatically in tandem with obesity. Today nearly 26 million Americans have diabetes. Worldwide, according to the United Nations, more than 350 million people worldwide have been diagnosed. The WHO estimates that type 2 diabetes comprises fully 90 percent of people with diabetes. This more common form of diabetes is largely the result of poor diet, physical inactivity, and weight gain. According to the American Diabetes Association, the nation spent $176 billion in direct medical costs to treat type 1 and type 2 diabetes in 2012, when the cost was last examined. On a global level, estimated health care costs for diabetes are between $376 billion and $670 billion. Because obesity significantly increases the risk of developing type 2 diabetes, many believe these astronomical costs could be largely reduced through preventive measures.

Aside from the health care expenditures, the loss of productivity in the workplace is costly. In general, loss of productivity includes absenteeism due to the inability to work as a result of obesity-related illness and disability and fewer productive working years due to early death. Job absenteeism related to obesity costs the nation an estimated $4.3 billion annually. Obesity is even related to lower productivity while at work, costing employers roughly $500 annually for each obese worker. A 2014 study by Virginia Tech and the University of Buffalo, for example, found that overweight and obese people are less efficient in completing tasks and need longer rest breaks than normal-weight employees. In addition, overweight and obese people have higher workers' compensation claims because, as the Virginia Tech and other studies have found, obese people are more likely to get injured on the job.

Obesity may even impact the nation's ability to defend itself, as roughly 27 percent of military applicants are being rejected because they are too overweight to fight. General John Shalikashvili, former chairman of the Joint Chiefs of Staff, considers obesity a threat to national security. According to Shalikashvili, "Every month hundreds of otherwise excellent candidates for military service are turned away by recruiters because of weight problems. Since 1995, the proportion of recruits who failed their physical exams because they were overweight has risen by nearly 70 percent."[10]

Clearly the problem of obesity has far-reaching effects that impact all levels of society. As Lisel Loy and Laura Zatz of the Bipartisan Policy Center put it,

> Obesity and chronic disease are not just health issues. They are economic and national security issues. They affect our kids and their performance in school. They affect the health of our businesses and the strength of our families and communities. Everyone, from employers and insurers to doctors and community health workers to governors and mayors to food retailers and manufacturers, has a role to play and a stake in the outcomes—improving health and cutting health care costs are essential to all of us.[11]

While the seriousness of the current trend cannot be overstated, there is some encouraging news. In the United States, the CDC reported in 2013 that obesity rates among preschool children from low-income families had decreased in eighteen states, and adult obesity rates, while still too high, had remained fairly level in most states. Nevertheless, experts state that the country has yet to record real and lasting progress. The US Department of Health and Human Services (HHS) has set a goal to reduce adult obesity rates from 33.9 percent to 30.5 percent by the year 2020. Whether the nation—and world—will succeed in turning back the obesity epidemic remains to be seen.

"Obesity and chronic disease are not just health issues. They are economic and national security issues."[11]

—Bipartisan Policy Center analysts Lisel Loy and Laura Zatz.

Should Government Regulate Access to Junk Food?

As obesity continues to sweep across the nation, many researchers are starting to examine to what extent food environment factors—such as the proximity of fast-food outlets, the availability of grocery stores, food prices, and other community characteristics—play a role in the food choices people make. Many health advocates argue that the entire food environment has been completely transformed in the last several decades. Today processed and fast foods served in huge portions—the types of foods usually associated with weight gain—are cheap and available virtually anywhere in the country. Access to so much junk food, many believe, has driven the obesity epidemic, and prevention efforts must focus on improving food environments so that consumers are not constantly bombarded with enticements to eat unhealthy foods.

Christina Roberto, assistant professor of social and behavioral sciences and nutrition at the Harvard T.H. Chan School of Public Health, is among those who believe that the current food environment is one of the major barriers restricting progress in controlling the obesity epidemic. A 2015 paper by Roberto and her colleagues states,

> While we need to acknowledge that individuals bear some responsibility for their health, we also need to recognize that today's food environments exploit people's vulnerabilities and make it easier to eat unhealthy foods. . . . This reinforces preferences and demands for foods of poor nutritional quality, leading to environmental changes that further encourage consumption of unhealthy foods.[12]

Deborah A. Cohen, a natural scientist at the RAND Corporation, puts it even more simply: "The modern food environment is the largest determinant of our behavior—and what we need to focus on if we are going to end the obesity epidemic."[13]

Fast Food and Obesity

Fast food, in particular, has come under increased scrutiny for its role in the obesity epidemic, primarily because it is calorie dense, nutrient poor, and served in large, inexpensive portions. Since 1970 the number of fast-food restaurants has doubled. Today more than three hundred thousand fast-food outlets operate in America, and consumers spend more than $100 billion dollars a year purchasing these foods.

Public health officials note that obesity rates have skyrocketed in tandem with the proliferation of fast-food establishments in shopping malls, schools, stadiums, and even hospitals. When a McDonald's or Taco Bell lurks around every corner, critics say, choosing unhealthy food is all too easy. A disproportionate number of these establishments, moreover, is located near elementary schools and in low-income areas; the convenience and affordability of these foods may lure children and other consumers into making unhealthy choices.

> "Policies restricting access to fast food near schools could have significant effects on obesity among school children."[14]
>
> —National Bureau of Economic Research.

An ongoing study titled *The Effect of Fast Food Restaurants on Obesity* bears this out. As part of the study, researchers are collecting data in an attempt to determine whether proximity to fast-food restaurants affects the obesity rates of 3 million schoolchildren. The authors report that having a fast-food restaurant within .10 miles (.16 km) of a school increases the risk of obesity by 5.2 percent, although there is no increased effect if the fast food is .25 or .50 miles (.40 or .80 km) from a school. The researchers examined whether other types of restaurants affected children's obesity rates. They did not. The authors conclude that "policies restricting access to fast food near schools could have significant effects on obesity among school children."[14]

Zoning Laws

One way to restrict access to these types of foods involves zoning laws, which limit the density of fast-food restaurants in par-

A 2015 study suggests that while soda, candy, and fast food are not beneficial to health, they are not significantly related to weight gain. To effectively combat obesity, it's more important to address the overall diet and level of physical activity than to restrict specific foods.

ticular areas. For example, zoning laws can establish buffer zones between schools and fast-food restaurants, convenience stores, and other establishments that sell junk food. Supporters of zoning laws argue that these types of laws have successfully reduced the negative effects of problem drinking. Although they differ from state to state, alcohol zoning ordinances are typically used to restrict the number and location of alcohol retailers. Studies show

Kids and Teachers Protest School Lunch Restrictions

The Healthy, Hunger-Free Kids Act of 2010 reduced the calories in public school lunches. Students and teachers from a high school in Kansas created a YouTube parody to protest these restrictions. The video, titled "We Are Hungry," is a parody of the song "We Are Young."

Give me some seconds, I need to get some food today

My friends are at the corner store getting junk so they don't
    waste away

My lover ate two grams of meat, just bout to starve

My bread was taken by some school bully asking about some more

I know I gave up on food months ago

I know I'm trying to forget

But between the milk and feta cheese the pains in my tummy sing,
    you know

I'm trying hard to find nourishment

So if by the time you go to practice and you feel like falling down

I'll carry you home

Chorus:

Tonight, we are hungry

Set the policy on fire

It can burn brighter than the sun

The Young Turks, "'We Are Hungry' Parody Video on Michelle Obama School Lunches," YouTube, September 26, 2012. www.youtube.com.

that the areas that reduced the density of alcohol retailers also reduced the incidence of alcohol-related automobile accidents and violence as well as negative health effects, such as cirrhosis of the liver. Because regulating alcohol accessibility has been so effective in reducing these and other problems related to drinking, many believe that regulating food accessibility is a promising way to control obesity.

Zoning laws are not without detractors, however. Critics point to food zoning ordinances in Los Angeles and other cities that failed to curb obesity rates. In 2008, for example, Los Angeles passed a zoning ordinance that restricted the expansion of fast-food outlets in one of its poorest sections, South Los Angeles,

Widespread Support for Healthy School Lunches

Debra Eschmeyer is the senior policy adviser for nutrition policy under the Obama administration. Here, she puts forth research and polls that show strong support for the updated school lunch standards. These findings, Eschmeyer says, "show that the updated school meal standards are working, and that we need to continue the great work happening in schools to provide students with nutritious meals."

A poll by the W.K. Kellogg Foundation this summer [2015] showed 9 out of 10 Americans feel nutrition standards in schools are important, with 86 percent saying that the current standards should stay in place or be made stronger.

A study published earlier this year in *Childhood Obesity* found that the updated standards were not contributing to plate waste, and that more students chose to take fruit and students consumed more of the vegetables they took in their meals.

A poll released by the Pew Charitable Trusts, Robert Wood Johnson Foundation, and the American Heart Association in the fall of 2014 showed 91 percent of parents support requiring schools to include a serving of fruits or vegetables with every meal.

A survey of school leaders from July 2014 showcased widespread student acceptance of the healthier lunches after the nutrition standards went into effect.

Debra Eschmeyer, "New Study Shows Students Selecting Healthier School Meals After Implementation of Updated Nutrition Standards," *Let's Move* (blog), January 4, 2016. www.letsmove.gov.

an area marked with disproportionately high obesity rates. The RAND Corporation conducted a study to examine whether this particular mandate improved public health. As Roland Sturm, a RAND economist, sums up, "It had no meaningful effect. There is no evidence that diets have improved more in South L.A. Obesity and overweight rates have not fallen."[15] Researchers speculate that this may be, in part, because the healthy options in grocery stores are much more expensive than the price of convenience food or fast food, making these options more desirable—even if more distant to reach—to people counting their pennies.

In light of such failures, critics charge that the government should not mandate how and where fast food is sold and served. A body of research appears to support this view, as a number of studies have been unable to firmly establish a causal link between fast food and obesity.

Looking at Overall Dietary Patterns

For example, a 2014 study out of the Gillings School of Global Public Health at the University of North Carolina at Chapel Hill examined a wide variety of factors that play a role in childhood obesity. According to Barry M. Popkin, a professor of global nutrition and the lead author of the study, what is really driving children's obesity is a pervasive dietary pattern—which includes high amounts of sweetened drinks and processed foods and few fruits and vegetables—that is fostered by children's parents or other caregivers. It is this that must be addressed in any meaningful solution. According to Popkin and his colleagues, "Eating fast foods is just one behavior that results from those bad habits. Just because children who eat more fast food are the most likely to become obese does not prove that calories from fast foods bear the brunt of the blame."[16]

Another 2015 study similarly concludes that antiobesity efforts that hinge on the vilification of certain foods are misguided and that attempting to keep these foods out of the hands of consumers is a waste of time and money. This study, conducted at the Cornell University Food and Brand Lab, focuses specifically on soda, candy, and fast food, which are often regarded as primary instigators of obesity. This new research reports that although these foods are certainly not beneficial to health, they are not significantly related to weight gain. As lead researcher David R. Just says, "This means that diets and health campaigns aimed at reducing and preventing obesity may be off track if they hinge on demonizing specific foods. If we want real change we need to look at the overall diet, and physical activity. Narrowly targeting junk foods is not just ineffective, it may be self-defeating as it distracts from the real underlying causes of obesity."[17]

On the other hand, supporters of measures to limit access to fast food contend that change will not happen overnight; rather, it will likely take years to see health gains after anti–junk food laws are put in place. Gwen Flynn of the Community Health Councils, which supported the Los Angeles zoning ordinance, believes even small victories matter. Commenting on the failure in South Los Angeles, Flynn says, "We never said this ordinance was the silver bullet [to solving the obesity epidemic]. . . . As long as we can make sure that people have more options, that's the important thing."[18]

> "Diets and health campaigns aimed at reducing and preventing obesity may be off track if they hinge on demonizing specific foods."[17]
>
> —David R. Just, professor at Cornell University and codirector of the Cornell Center for Behavioral Economics in Child Nutrition Programs.

Giving Consumers More Options

The USDA, in conjunction with Policy Map, a web-based organization that maps data related to health and other demographics, measures food accessibility in different communities. Data show that income level determines, in part, the types of food available to consumers. Whereas people in low-income neighborhoods generally have limited access to supermarkets selling wholesome, affordable food, residents of high-income neighborhoods, especially those in big cities, have access to a much wider array of fresh produce and other healthy foods. In New York City, for example, 72 percent of residents live within a five-minute walk of a well-stocked grocery store. On the other hand, researchers found

Residents of high-income neighborhoods, especially those in big cities, have access to a wide array of fresh produce and other healthy foods, while people in low-income neighborhoods generally have limited access to supermarkets selling wholesome, affordable food.

that residents in poorer areas had less access to supermarkets and healthy food in general.

A study by the Reinvestment Fund concludes that an estimated 24.6 million Americans live in these so-called food deserts where affordable, nutritious food is difficult to obtain. Many doctors and other public health officials find these statistics troubling, as individuals may opt for less nutritious options if healthy foods are not available. According to a joint study from the University of Illinois and the University of Michigan, access to a large supermarket is associated with a lower BMI in teens. In contrast, easy access to fast food in huge portions and convenience stores with aisles of tasty processed foods is associated with a higher BMI. As Temple University public health professor Jennifer Fisher says, "We know that the prospect of maintaining self-control in this environment is fairly grim." Fisher goes on to say that "to promote self-regulation, you have to constrain the environment in a way that makes the healthy choice the easy choice."[19] The easy choice, for many people, is fast food.

Healthy Food Financing Initiative

To boost access to healthier foods, a number of organizations and policy makers are seeking novel ways to place supermarkets and farmers' markets into economically distressed neighborhoods that suffer high rates of obesity. At the federal level, the Healthy Food Financing Initiative, launched in 2010, funds programs that seek to attract supermarkets and other healthy food venues to underserved communities. Kathleen Sebelius, the former HHS secretary, explains why these initiatives are important: "Encouraging people to choose fresh, nutritious food is important. But to achieve that goal that kind of food must be available, and in far too many parts of our country—both urban and rural communities—that's not the case. This collaborative initiative is a creative way to help solve that problem."[20]

State and local governments are also funding programs that offer financing and other incentives to improve food quality in areas with a large proportion of obese residents. One program that brings healthy foods into impoverished areas is New York's Bed-Stuy Campaign Against Hunger. Program participants build organic farms where residents diagnosed with obesity or diabetes can obtain high-quality vegetables, fruits, and eggs. Another program in New York is Communities for Healthy Food, which brings public gardens, free cooking classes, and farmers' markets to communities that need them. One young boy who is part of a program called the Bronx Helpers, which distributes healthy snacks to rush-hour commuters, says that before he became involved with the program, "Whenever I got money . . . I would buy a bag of chips and an Arizona [iced tea]."[21] Now he is part of the changing movement toward healthier options.

Despite these successes, a body of research indicates that these programs may not be enough to significantly alter people's eating habits or decrease obesity rates. Researchers from the University of North Carolina tracked thousands of people in several large cities over a fifteen-year period. The study found that people didn't eat more produce and other healthy foods even when they had access to supermarkets in their neighborhoods. Researchers did find, however, that having fast food restaurants nearby did increase consumption of fast-food among certain groups, including lower-income men, suggesting that proximity to fast-food restaurants was a stronger factor in food choice. What's more, even giving consumers access to supermarkets that sell plenty of fresh fruits and vegetables can have unintended consequences. Cohen describes a Kroger's Food 4 Less, a chain store that sells reasonably priced produce and other healthy options but also inundates consumers with countless varieties of junk foods:

> Right at the entrance one must run a gauntlet of cases and cases of juices, Chips Ahoy cookies, Coca-Cola, Sprite, Sunkist orange soda, Squirt, and 7Up stacked high. . . . As you move through the store, the end aisle displays contain more Coca-Cola and Chips Ahoy, along with Cup Noodles, BBQ chips, doughnuts, Cap'n Crunch, Pepsi, Orange Crush, Mountain Dew, and Doritos, not to mention aisles devoted exclusively to more chips and sodas. In the front of the store, before you approach the area for checkout, there are special displays of M&M's, single-serving packages of pastries, Reese's candies, and Nestle Crunch bars. And if your diet goals weren't already hijacked, there is an extensive display of candy bars and smaller bags of chips right next to the cash register, at about eye level for a seven-year-old.[22]

As Penny Gordon-Larsen, lead researcher of the University of North Carolina study, sums up, "No single approach, such as just having access to fresh fruits and veggies, might be effective in changing the way people eat. We really need to look at numerous ways of changing diet behaviors. There are likely more effective ways to influence what people eat."[23]

Limiting Junk Food in Schools

Most health care professionals contend that childhood is a critical time for obesity prevention, as eating habits formed in childhood are likely to persist into adulthood. Today an estimated 55 million American children attend elementary or secondary school, where they spend, on average, six hours a day. Most will eat at least one meal at school, along with snacks. Many believe that strong nutrition standards in schools may help turn around climbing obesity rates.

In 2010 the Healthy, Hunger-Free Kids Act allowed the USDA to update nutrition standards in schools for the first time in fifteen years, promoting the adoption of healthier lunches that include fruits and vegetables and limiting foods like tater tots and pizza.

Improving the nutritional standards at schools is the focal point of the Healthy, Hunger-Free Kids Act of 2010. The act, which gave the USDA the authority to update nutrition standards in schools for the first time in fifteen years, promotes the adoption of healthier lunches that include fruits and vegetable and limit foods like tater tots and pizza. It also established minimum and maximum amounts of calories in school-provided lunches. Today close to 97 percent of schools are implementing these new standards. In addition, federal guidelines announced in 2013 mandate that snacks sold during school hours—in vending machines or à la carte lines—must meet federal nutrition guidelines.

> "We cannot simply bully kids into eating healthful foods and take their lunch money."[24]
>
> —David R. Just and Brian Wansink, professors at Cornell University and codirectors of the Cornell Center for Behavioral Economics in Child Nutrition Programs.

A number of reports suggest these initiatives are working. A 2016 study published in *JAMA Pediatrics* reviewed the nutritional content of roughly 1.7 million school lunches selected by students before and after the new standards took effect. Researchers found that students picked healthier foods as a result of the updated standards. These positive changes, researchers report, were likely driven by the increased availability of fruits, vegetables, and other healthy foods.

Banning Junk Food May Backfire

On the other hand, critics say studies like these don't tell the complete story. They contend that nutritional standards can backfire because many students choose to go hungry rather than eat the healthy fare offered. David R. Just and Brian Wansink, professors at Cornell University and codirectors of the Cornell Center for Behavioral Economics in Child Nutrition Programs, argue that children will not eat food they don't like, even if that is the only food available in the lunch line. When radical changes are imposed, children may just wait to binge on junk food after school. Just and Wansink describe what happened when Los Angeles took a hard line limiting the availability of the foods typically served to students:

In an attempt to mold better eating habits in kids, the Los Angeles Unified School District eliminated flavored milk, chicken nuggets and other longtime childhood favorites. But instead of making kids healthier, the changes sent students fleeing from school cafeterias. There have been reports of a thriving trade in black-market junk food, of pizzas delivered to side doors and of family-sized bags of chips being brought from home. Garbage cans are filling up with the more nutritious foods, even if kids aren't. . . . The lesson? We cannot simply bully kids into eating healthful foods and take their lunch money.[24]

Just and Wansick conclude that the government should think twice about limiting the availability of unhealthy foods because "when children (or even adults) feel restricted or forced into a decision, they naturally rebel."[25] Instead of limiting certain foods, these and other experts argue, a better choice may be guiding and educating consumers so that they make healthier decisions when it comes to what to eat.

Can Educational Programs Help Control Obesity?

The notion that obesity is primarily the result of individual lifestyle choices—poor diet and physical inactivity, for example—has long been part of the national debate about the problem. David A. Kessler is a pediatrician concerned with rising obesity rates. He also served as the commissioner of the USDA under George H.W. Bush and Bill Clinton and has been the dean of the medical schools at Yale and the University of California, San Francisco. Kessler believes that the cultural messages that influence eating behavior encourage unhealthy lifestyles that favor the development of obesity. In today's world, for example, consuming a 42-ounce (1.2 L) soda in one sitting is commonplace; round-the-clock snacking, super-sized meals, and sedentary lifestyles are also becoming the norm.

The solution, according to Kessler and others, is a system of well-funded education campaigns that change individual behavior and enable new social norms to emerge. Kessler says, "That's what happened with tobacco—the attitudes that created the social acceptability of smoking shifted, and many of us began to see smoking as deviant, and even repulsive, behavior." To redefine social norms that govern food intake, Kessler says, people need "to hear repeatedly, from many sources, that selling, serving, and eating food layered with sugar, fat, and salt has negative, unhealthy consequences."[26] This idea—that antiobesity efforts should focus on educating and enabling consumers so that they change the behaviors that lead to weight gain—has led to an array of federal, state, and local programs that many hope will have a meaningful impact on the current epidemic.

MyPlate

The cornerstone of many federal and local nutrition education programs is the *Dietary Guidelines for Americans*, a report put forth jointly by the USDA and HHS. It is revised every five years based on a review of the latest scientific and medical research. The resulting guidelines contain nutritional information and recommendations to help all individuals ages two and over consume a nutritionally sound diet that promotes healthy weight. The latest dietary guidelines for 2015 through 2020 encourage Americans to eat fewer calories, less sugar, and more fruits and vegetables. The USDA helps prioritize food choices by using the familiar image of a plate. This visual icon, called MyPlate, reminds consumers to make half of their plate fruits and vegetables, with smaller portions of protein, whole grains, and dairy.

In addition to driving policy decisions, such as what kinds of foods public schools serve students, MyPlate provides the basis for much of the nutrition education materials designed for the public. Because most experts believe that the foundation of good health begins in childhood—and indeed, the CDC reports that overweight children are more likely to be overweight adults—many educational interventions today focus on the youngest members of society. Schools, therefore, may have one of the richest opportunities to reach a large swath of the nation's youth before obesity sets in.

> "We should expect schools to teach children about food—where it comes from and how it affects our bodies and our health."[27]
>
> —Michael F. Jacobson, executive director of the Center for Science in the Public Interest.

Michael F. Jacobson is the executive director of the Center for Science in the Public Interest (CSPI), a consumer advocacy organization that provides consumers and policy makers with information related to food and health. Jacobson would like to see food education in every classroom. He says,

Some American school kids cannot identify tomatoes, beets, or cauliflower, or might mistake an eggplant for a pear! Yet thanks to Big Food's marketing muscle, junk food brands like McDonald's, Coca-Cola, and Chuck E. Cheese's are firmly implanted in kids' developing brains. . . . Just as we expect our schools to do the heavy lifting when it comes to teaching geography, algebra, physical education, and history, we should expect schools to teach children about food—where it comes from and how it affects our bodies and our health.[27]

First Lady Michelle Obama plays table tennis during a Let's Move! event in New York City. The First Lady's Let's Move! program focuses on nutrition education and better food labeling, and encourages people to get moving through regular exercise.

To this end, schools across the country participate in a variety of nutrition programs, such as Fruits and Veggies: More Matters. This program teaches children the importance of eating more fruits and vegetables, which play an important role in combating obesity and preventing many diet-related diseases, including heart disease, diabetes, and stroke. Team Nutrition is a similar program of the USDA. It distributes nutrition education materials to children, schools, and community resources to support healthy eating.

Let's Move!

One of the most well-known initiatives is First Lady Michelle Obama's Let's Move! program, which was launched in 2010. It is "dedicated to solving the challenge of childhood obesity within a generation, so that children born today will grow up healthier and able to pursue their dreams,"[28] according to the program's goals. Let's Move! focuses, in part, on nutrition education in classrooms, better food labeling, and the provision of educational materials to parents and caregivers so that they too have the tools to raise normal-weight children. As the name implies, the program also strives to get people moving through regular exercise.

To spread her message, the First Lady often takes to the public stage. She has appeared dancing on comedian Jimmy Fallon's talk show, has hopped through the White House in a potato sack, and has appeared with two Muppets—Elmo and Rosita—at a news conference to talk about getting kids to eat more fruits and vegetables. She even created a video in which she dances with a turnip to the popular hit song, "Turn Down for What." In her quest to connect with children and help them eat better and be more active, Obama says, "I'm pretty much willing to make a complete fool of myself."[29]

Most obesity researchers agree that it is difficult to know if, or to what extent, these programs are having a noticeable effect on rising obesity levels. As the CDC reports, obesity rates among two- to five-year-olds have declined by roughly 40 percent since 2003. While there are likely multiple reasons for this decrease, some observers speculate that Let's Move! is one of them. Although Obama herself concedes that the country has a long way to go to transform the health of an entire generation, she says, "Make no mistake about it, we are changing the conversation in this country. . . . We are creating a cultural shift in how we live and eat and our efforts are beginning to have a real impact on our children's lives."[30]

Mixed Support for Healthy Eating Educational Initiatives

Others contend that although the decreases in the youngest age group are a positive sign, obesity rates in youth or adults during the same time period have not budged, leaving little evidence that these efforts work—or merit the high price tag attached to them. Let's Move! alone costs over a billion dollars a year to administer.

Others oppose costly government interventions on the grounds that children should be taught the value of fresh, wholesome foods and other healthy habits from parents, who are ultimately responsible for a child's weight.

Many home environments don't encourage healthy eating, however. Robert H. Lustig argues that the forces that lead to childhood obesity—unhealthy home environments, the ubiquity of junk food, food marketing that targets children—are extremely powerful and impossible to fight with a nutrition program, even an expensive one. Lustig compares nutrition education to interventions that targeted recreational drugs:

> For alcohol, tobacco, and street drugs, most of the popular approaches to public health education don't work to curtail abuse for two reasons: because they do not do anything to reduce availability of the substance in question, and because those substances are addictive. For instance, school-based education programs have little effect on reducing alcohol consumption. School-based obesity education programs to date also show limited success, in part because our kids' food preferences are formed before they ever get to school and because their home environment remains constant. Teaching the child won't fix her environment. . . . Ask the fat kid who returns from fat camp and gains all his weight back within three months.[31]

It remains unlikely that public health campaigns that focus on getting people to eat right will single-handedly solve the obesity crisis. Besides, many critics say, Big Macs and french fries are not the sole drivers of today's soaring obesity rates; the remote control and e-mail may be as much to blame.

Sedentary Lifestyles

According to a report issued by the Institute of Medicine (IOM), most adults and children need to exercise at least an hour a day to stay healthy. Studies consistently show, however, that Americans have become much less physically active in recent decades. For example, researchers from Stanford University examined health survey data from 1988 through 2010 and found huge increases in inactivity. Over this time period, the percentage of inactive men increased from 11 percent to 43 percent; the percentage for inactive women surged from 19 percent to 52 percent. According to Uri Ladabaum, an associate professor of gastroenterology at Stanford and the lead author of the study, "What struck us the most was just how dramatic the change in leisure-time physical activity was."[32] Ladabaum and his colleagues conclude that today's plummeting levels of inactivity are behind the huge increases in obesity.

In recent decades people have become much less physically active, which has contributed to the obesity problem. These changes are partly due to the explosion of technological advances—computers and tablets, for example—that lead to more sedentary lifestyles.

Falsely Pinning the Blame for Obesity on Lack of Exercise

British cardiologist Aseem Malhotra and colleagues express their view that physical activity does not prevent obesity.

Many still wrongly believe that obesity is entirely due to lack of exercise. This false perception is rooted in the Food Industry's Public Relations machinery, which uses tactics chillingly similar to those of big tobacco. The tobacco industry successfully stalled government intervention for 50 years starting from when the first links between smoking and lung cancer were published. This sabotage was achieved using a "corporate playbook" of denial, doubt and confusing the public. . . .

Coca Cola, who spent $3.3 billion on advertising in 2013, pushes a message that "all calories count"; they associate their products with sports, suggesting that it is okay to consume their drinks as long as you exercise.

Aseem Malhotra et al., "It Is Time to Bust the Myth of Physical Inactivity and Obesity: You Cannot Outrun a Bad Diet," *British Journal of Sports Medicine*, April 22, 2015. http://bjsm.bmj.com.

These changes are partly due to the explosion of technological advances—computers and televisions, for example—that lead to more sedentary lifestyles. Today more than 40 percent of children watch two or more hours of television each day, and many forms of work require employees to sit in front of a computer screen for eight hours a day. Medical writer Chris Woolston describes how these modern conveniences put fewer physical demands on people:

At work, we point and click instead of sweat and toil. And when work is done, we have every opportunity to take it easy. Why walk to the post office when you can drive? Why walk around the mall when you can shop online? Why throw around a football when you can play NFL 2004 on your X-box? In addition, many of our towns aren't exactly conducive to walking. Who wants to stroll over to the nearest shopping center if you have to walk across a culvert and a freeway to get there?[33]

To circumvent these trends, Let's Move! and other community programs strive to educate individuals about the benefits of adopting and maintaining an active lifestyle. Many urban centers

Falsely Pinning the Blame for Obesity on Food Intake

Coca-Cola's position paper on obesity, from which the following is excerpted, puts forth the company's view that all foods and beverages can be part of a healthy, active lifestyle.

Obesity is a serious and complex global health challenge that affects individuals in every culture, community, and country around the world. . . .

There is wide spread consensus that weight gain is primarily the result of an imbalance of energy—specifically too many calories consumed versus expended.

When it comes to managing weight, it's important to balance calories consumed with calories burned—what the experts refer to as energy balance. This is a simple concept with deceptively complex dynamics.

People consume many different foods and beverages, so no single food or beverage alone is responsible for the obesity crisis. But, when it comes to weight management, all calories count, whatever food or beverage they come from, including those from our beverages.

We recognize the uniqueness of consumers' lifestyles and dietary choices. All of our products can be part of an active, healthy lifestyle that includes a sensible, balanced diet, proper hydration, and regular, physical activity.

Coca-Cola Company, "Our Position on Obesity," December 2013. www.coca-colacompany.com.

and other areas, however, are bereft of playing fields, gyms, and outdoor areas that foster physical activity, making it difficult for residents to exercise and maintain healthy habits. The development of community spaces that encourage physical activity, many argue, must go hand in hand with educational campaigns that promote regular physical activity.

Increasing Opportunities for Exercise

Let's Move! aims to "increase opportunities for kids to be physically active, both in and out of school, and to create new opportunities for families to move together."[34] These goals are in line with recommendations by the CDC, the WHO, the IOM, and other health organizations, which recommend that schools provide a total of 150 minutes of physical education per week for elementary schoolchildren and 225 minutes per week for middle and high school students. Schools are encouraged to ensure that children spend most of this time being active.

> "At work, we point and click instead of sweat and toil. And when work is done, we have every opportunity to take it easy. Why walk to the post office when you can drive? Why walk around the mall when you can shop online?"[33]
>
> —Medical writer Chris Woolston.

Another national goal is the development of walking and biking paths that can be used for leisure activities and for commuting to school. The McKinsey Global Institute reports that in 1969 roughly 40 percent of children walked or rode a bike to school. By 2001, this figure dropped to 13 percent. The national Safe Routes to School (SRTS) program was established by Congress in 2005 to address these trends. The program distributes federal funds so that states can improve safety on walking and biking routes to school so that children and adults will be more likely to use these modes. Importantly, SRTS guides states in educating and encouraging individuals to actively commute. Between 2005 and 2009, SRTS distributed $1.15 billion across all fifty states and Washington, DC, to support these projects. A 2015 study at the University of North Carolina at Chapel Hill reported that the SRTS program had increased the number of students who biked or walked to school, although it remains difficult to measure whether increased physical fitness will translate into reduced obesity rates.

Many observers argue that even biking to school and extra gym classes may not be enough to counterbalance the overconsumption of calories that is typical in today's food environment. Although figures vary according to a person's BMI and other individual attributes, nutritionists have a rough idea of how much exercise is required to burn particular foods. A Big Mac combo meal, for example, would require six straight hours of walking to burn off; likewise, a person would have to walk for fifty-five minutes to burn off the calories in a can of Coca-Cola or run for over fifty minutes to work off a Hershey's chocolate bar.

What's more, even getting kids to walk to school may have unintended consequences. Kristen Madsen, an obesity researcher at the UCB School of Public Health, showed, for example, that kids who walk to school sometimes gain weight because they have to pass fast-food restaurants and other junk food outlets on their way home.

Portion Control and Menu Labeling

According to the National Restaurant Association, Americans are eating at restaurants an average of four times per week. In fact, Americans consume an estimated one-third of their daily calories while dining out. Many health advocates believe it's no coincidence that obesity levels are rising while Americans are eating out in record numbers. Studies consistently demonstrate that the consumption of restaurant food, whether fast food or from a more expensive dining establishment, is linked to weight problems and obesity.

One reason why restaurants may cause weight gain is that food portions have swelled dramatically in recent years. At the same time, restaurant offerings are usually filled with fat, sugar, and other highly caloric ingredients. As a result, consumers— even the most well intentioned—may consume more calories

Studies show that the consumption of restaurant food is linked to weight problems and obesity. One reason is that food portions have swelled dramatically in recent years and, as a result, even the most well-intentioned diners may consume more calories than they realize.

than they realize. To educate consumers and boost awareness, the CSPI publishes some of the most egregious examples of unhealthy restaurant fare: The Louisiana Chicken Pasta at the popular chain the Cheesecake Factory weighs in at 2,370 calories, the center reports. Outback Steakhouse's Herb Roasted Prime

Rib meal with a potato and salad contains 2,400 calories, and IHOP's Chorizo Fiesta Omelette meal contains 1,990 calories. As the CSPI says of this IHOP breakfast,

> A 1,300 calorie sausage omelette alone would strike many as a tad on the heavy side. But this one comes with three buttermilk pancakes (or hash browns, toast, or fruit, but this is IHOP, after all). Remember when three pancakes alone was a big breakfast?
>
> Add four tablespoons of syrup, and you shuffle out with a day's calories (1,990). . . . You might as well have ordered a McDonald's Big Breakfast (scrambled eggs, hash browns, biscuit, and sausage) with three Sausage McMuffins and five packets of grape jam on the side.[35]

Since 1990, the Nutritional Labeling and Education Act has required nutritional information posted on packaged foods. A number of health advocates have called for similar initiatives to help diners navigate today's restaurant offerings and make more informed choices about what they are ordering. In response, Congress passed a national menu labeling law in 2010. It requires all chain restaurants with twenty or more outlets to display calorie counts on menus and menu boards. Today movie theaters, sports stadiums, and other food sellers are also required to provide calorie information to consumers. In addition to educating consumers, proponents argue, menu labeling will prompt food companies to reformulate healthier options.

The CSPI is a strong supporter of these types of programs that encourage healthy eating away from home: "Without clear, easy-to-use nutrition information at the point of ordering, it's difficult to make informed and healthy choices."[36] Some evidence suggests menu labeling may be impacting consumer choices. A study from Starbucks found that customers selected food purchases with 14 percent fewer calories after the store started menu labeling; another survey by NPD, a company that tracks consumer spending, reported that consumers ordered less junk food when ordering from a labeled menu. At the same time, however, a 2013 study out of Carnegie Mellon and Cornell Universities that examined what foods New York diners ate before and after menu labeling rules went into effect reported that "posting calorie benchmarks had no direct impact . . . on food purchases."[37]

With so many conflicting studies, it is too soon to draw definitive conclusions regarding the efficacy of menu labeling. As nutrition researcher Joanne Arsenault says,

> One could argue that the entire U.S. population has been exposed to nutrition labeling of foods for almost two decades and obesity is rising. Likewise, if obesity starts to decrease after mandatory labeling goes into effect, this does not infer causality. There are many other factors influencing obesity and a wide variety of efforts are being undertaken to tackle the obesity problem.[38]

Menu labeling and other initiatives that focus on personal behaviors are likely just some of the many interventions that will be tested as ways to encourage every citizen to adopt healthier behaviors.

Should the Marketing of Food to Children Be Restricted?

Marketing has long been part of America's food landscape. According to the Federal Trade Commission (FTC), today's food industry spends billions of dollars each year marketing its products to consumers young and old. Industry giants like the Kellogg Company, the world's leading producer of breakfast cereals and convenience foods, such as cookies, crackers, toaster pastries, and frozen waffles, spent over $1 billion in advertising in 2014. The Coca-Cola Company, makers of soft drinks, fruit juices, sports drinks, and other sweetened beverages, spent close to $3.5 billion in advertising the same year. A huge portion of these advertising dollars—over $2 billion a year—is aimed directly at the nation's youth. On top of this, the fast-food industry spends more than $5 million every day marketing its food to children and teens.

One of the primary ways advertisers reach children is through television. According to the Interagency Working Group on Foods Marketed to Children, children and adolescents see roughly four thousand televised food commercials each year. Nearly 98 percent of these ads feature fast foods or processed foods high in sugar, fat, and salt. The reach of food ads is much broader than television, however. Food ads also target children through radio, magazines, celebrity endorsements, toys, collectibles, clothing, contests, and games. Favorite cartoon media characters, such as SpongeBob or Shrek, and brand mascots, such as Tony the Tiger, are emblazoned on the packaging of many sugary cereals and unhealthy snack foods to further sway children's preferences. Junk food ads are even placed in movies and television shows: in the blockbuster movie *Home Alone,* for example, children watch fun scenes in which actors drink Pepsi.

Advertising in the Digital World

The explosion of the Internet in the 1990s extended the reach of food marketing in unprecedented ways. Today young people can interact with the brands they love using digital devices like smartphones and laptops. Because of their high levels of online and mobile media consumption, teenagers are prime targets for digital food marketers. Today's sophisticated technology enables marketers to create immersive experiences that are extremely popular. One of McDonald's popular advertising campaigns, for example, incorporated virtual technology whereby kids could log on and play games on an avatar website, receiving higher scores if they purchased Big Macs or Happy Meals that included special game codes. The company's sales increased 18 percent after this particular campaign.

A 2012 report published in the journal *Pediatric Clinics of North America* estimates that 6 million three- to eleven-year-olds play some type of virtual online game each month; advertisers shell out close to $1 billion a year marketing goods—primarily food and beverages—in this media landscape. These engaging, interactive games appear to build brand loyalties from an early age. The Kellogg Company is among the food giants to embrace these new marketing strategies. The company's 2008 annual report reflected the company's move to target the digital generation: "We are aggressively embracing digital media, which affords an efficient, cost-effective way to target specific audiences, providing an excellent platform for developing our brands. We have already tapped the Internet to gain significant brand development traction for *Special K, Frosted Flakes, Apple Jacks, Kashi, Rice Krispies, Morningstar Farms* and *Pop-Tarts.*"[39]

The Persuasive Power of Food Marketing

The reach of food marketing into the lives of the nation's youth is indeed broad. Michael F. Jacobson writes that it is also "wildly successful":

> Would you be surprised to know that there is a highly-sophisticated, multi-billion-dollar campaign underway designed to teach your children about food? There is. In fact, experts agree that this campaign is wildly successful. Unfortunately, the massive instructional campaign to which

I refer is the $2 billion effort by the food industry to teach children and teens to want candy, sugar drinks, sugary cereals, and other highly-processed junk foods.[40]

Many studies corroborate the persuasive power of food advertising. According to a review of studies by the IOM, a division of the National Academies of Science, Engineering, and Medicine, television food advertising strongly sways children's food

The Coca-Cola Company, makers of soft drinks, fruit juices, sports drinks, and other sweetened beverages, spent nearly $3.5 billion on advertising in 2014. More than half of those advertising dollars—over $2 billion—were aimed directly at the nation's youth.

Parents Find It Difficult to Control Their Kids' Eating Habits

Josh Scherer is an assistant editor at the online magazine *TakePart*. Here, Scherer recalls his childhood pursuit of the Happy Meal toy. Even though he was only eight, Scherer was able to purchase Happy Meals without his parent's consent, challenging the notion that parents are solely responsible for what children eat.

In 2000, McDonald's launched its fourth series of Teenie Beanies: a cobranded effort with toy maker Ty Inc. that transformed its fiended-over Beanie Babies into miniature Happy Meal stuffers.

At the time, my allowance was $4 per week, which left me about 35 cents short of being able to buy a kid's meal plus the $2 supplement for the premium plush toy. I recycled soda cans to earn the extra dough, and every Monday after school, I stopped in to get a cheeseburger, fries, an orange Hi-C drink (it had vitamins!), and whatever miniature don't-call-it-a-stuffed-animal was next on the list.

I knew my dad would've been mad if he found out, so I ditched the evidence in a Dumpster and ate dinner as if I hadn't consumed 700 calories two hours prior. . . .

By the time the Teenie Beanies were replaced with Yu-Gi-Oh cards or Beyblades or Tech Deks, I had clandestinely eaten tens of thousands of extra calories' worth of Happy Meals. Ty Inc., Ronald McDonald, and the scores of high-paid marketing executives had done their duty.

Josh Scherer, "Other Countries Restrict Predatory Junk-Food Ads, but America Won't Budge," *TakePart*, July 8, 2015. www.takepart.com.

preferences—and negatively affects overall health. Another study published in 2015 in *Obesity Reviews* reports that advertising that includes popular media characters like Nemo or Scooby-Doo, known as spokes-characters, is especially powerful. The American Medical Association also weighs in, reporting that children under eight years old are uniquely susceptible to advertising because they tend to accept marketing gimmicks as accurate and unbiased; young children, moreover, are not able to distinguish between a TV program and a commercial. A 2007 study even reported that a thirty-second commercial can sway the brand preferences of two-year-olds.

Parents Must Control Their Children's Eating Habits

Rea Frey is a nutrition specialist and certified personal trainer who believes parents are solely responsible for their children's health.

It's a finicky thing—being a parent. Choosing what your child eats, when they eat it, and how often they eat it. Kids have food allergies. Kids don't like vegetables. Kids beg for chicken nuggets. Kids don't go outside. Kids play video games. Kids throw temper tantrums and become obese and unhealthy. Kids eat fast food. Once per day. Twice per day. Occasionally. They crave hamburgers. They drink sodas. They get fat. They grow into obese adults. They get sick. They die prematurely. It is an epidemic that is completely reversible.

Where does it start? With the parents. I marvel at the way some parents let their child dictate meals. "Oh, Tommy will only eat macaroni and cheese and fish sticks." Really? Why does he like macaroni? How does he even know what a fish stick is? . . .

So, why is obesity in children at an all-time high? Because they are eating things they are introduced to. . . . They don't pop out of the womb saying, "Take me to McDonald's!"

Rea Frey, "Do Your Kids Eat Fast Food? Might as Well Hand Them Cigarettes and Whiskey!" *Chicago Now*, May 16, 2011. www.chicagonow.com.

The Children's Food and Beverage Advertising Initiative

As the obesity epidemic came under increased scrutiny in the early years of the twenty-first century, the IOM stepped in to determine whether food marketing was directly contributing to children's soaring weights. The IOM's report, issued in 2005, concluded that "food and beverage marketing practices puts children's long term health at risk. If America's children and youth are to develop eating habits that help them avoid early onset of diet-related chronic diseases, they have to reduce their intake of high-calorie, low-nutrient snacks, fast foods, and sweetened drinks, which make up a high proportion of the products marketed to them."[41] To this end, the IOM recommended that food and beverage companies work with government and other public health groups to establish standards for marketing to children.

In response to the IOM report, the Better Business Bureau launched the Children's Food and Beverage Advertising Initiative (CFBAI) in 2006. The CFBAI is a voluntary self-regulation program that encourages food companies to either forgo child-directed marketing or to "shift the mix of foods advertised to children under 12 to encourage healthier dietary choices and lifestyle choices,"[42] according to the group's website. Participants are also asked to limit the use of cartoon characters in advertising. Kellogg's, General Mills, PepsiCo and other industry leaders banded together and pledged to fulfill these goals.

Some progress has been made. Today McDonald's offers apple slices and milk with the Happy Meal, for example, and cereal companies like General Mills have reduced the sugar content in Cocoa Puffs and other top sellers. In addition, some companies appear to be spending fewer child-directed advertising dollars: In 2009, the FTC released a report finding that three years after the CFBAI took effect, food companies were spending 19.5 percent less money marketing food to children. As CFBAI director Elaine Kolish stated, "The program is working. Since 2006 when CFBAI was founded, more companies have joined, hundreds of foods have been improved or newly created to meet science-based nu-

As childhood obesity levels have risen, the food industry has come under increased pressure to encourage healthier dietary choices for children. In 2011 McDonald's began offering apple slices and milk with its Happy Meal.

trition criteria, and the CFBAI itself has expanded and become even more rigorous."[43]

Opponents counter that more sweeping change is needed. Aside from some small improvements in food quality, a number of studies show that the marketing of junk food to children continues almost unabated. A study funded by the California Endowment found that despite self-regulation, 72.5 percent of the foods advertised on children's television shows were of the poorest nutritional quality. According to the Campaign for a Commercial-Free Child-hood (CCFC), moreover, ads for unhealthy foods decreased very little between the time self-regulation went into effect in 2005 and 2009, from 90 percent to 80 percent respectively.

Furthermore, character tie-ins remain widely used, despite food and beverage industry pledges to limit their use. A study by Children Now, an advocacy organization dedicated to improv-ing children's health and well-being, concluded the use of popu-lar children's characters like SpongeBob to advertise unhealthy foods actually increased after the inception of the CFBAI: Be-tween 2005 and 2009 the use of these characters increased from 8.8 percent to 15.2 percent.

In short, opponents contend, CFBAI's voluntary nutrition stan-dards and similar efforts are no match for the powerful and ubiq-uitous food marketers that continue to exploit "every technology and technique available to insinuate its brands into the fabric of childhood,"[44] as the CCFC says. One tactic used by the food industry, according to these critics, is to mislead consumers with claims that reformulated options are "healthy."

Marketing Versus Personal Responsibility

Bonnie Liebman, director of nutrition for the CSPI, comments on some of the healthy claims made by the breakfast cereal industry: "Companies take a junky cereal with a lot of sugar and add fiber to make parents think it's healthy for their kids. . . . If one-third of the bowl is sugar, it's breakfast candy."[45] Robert H. Lustig goes on to say that all the voluntary nutrition standards in the world won't fix the incessant and sophisticated marketing campaigns employed by industry giants:

> McDonald's now advertises a healthier menu, with com-mercials featuring slim people in exercise clothes eating salads. However, the vast majority of people entering Mc-Donald's, even if they come in with the idea of eating a salad, instead order a Big Mac and fries. And McDonald's is well aware of this. Its recent billboard campaign, "Craft-ed for Your Craving," says all you need to know. Carl's

Jr.'s promotion of the "Western Bacon Six Dollar Burger," which has a whopping 1,030 calories and 55 grams of fat, generally depicts fit and attractive people consuming the company's fare with relish. Do you really think they would continue to be thin if they ate this on a regular basis?[46]

On the other hand, many support the view that eating a burger—even if contains over a thousand calories—is a personal right that should be protected. The Center for Consumer Freedom (CCF) is a consumer watchdog group devoted to protecting the individual's right to choose what to eat and drink. According to the CCF, the connection between food advertising and obesity is weak, and "Americans have been force-fed a diet of bloated statistics hyping the problem of obesity. Those statistics have been used . . . to justify a host of noxious 'solutions.'"[47] Antimarketing forces, the CCF maintains, not only usurp consumer rights but also "fail to make people skinny." The CCF explains that "most advertising is aimed at turning consumers of one product to a similar product, like one soft drink brand to another. Ads are not primarily creating new soft-drink drinkers or snack eaters. Thus, it shouldn't be surprising that restricting advertising doesn't make people stop drinking soda or eating snacks."[48] The fact that a huge proportion of these low-nutrition foods and sugary beverages are advertised to young people—and influencing their eating habits—does not sway these critics, who believe that marketers are just responding to consumer demand.

> "The vast majority of people entering McDonald's, even if they come in with the idea of eating a salad, instead order a Big Mac and fries."[46]
>
> —Robert H. Lustig, a pediatric endocrinologist and expert on childhood obesity.

First Amendment Issues

Groups like the CCF and others also maintain that the First Amendment—which says that Congress cannot pass laws that abridge the freedom of speech—gives food and beverage companies the right to market foods any way they like. But with nearly a third of children and teenagers overweight or obese, many argue that these free speech protections should not apply to companies that target children with products that contribute to obesity. Susan Linn was a founding director of the CCFC from 2000 through 2015. According to Linn, "Free speech is not a blank check; it has limits. Current federal law actually prohibits unfair or deceptive advertising. . . . Marketing to children does not get First Amendment protection because it is inherently misleading. If a young child cannot even understand the purpose of an ad, then marketing anything to that child is both unfair and deceptive."[49]

> "Kids eat what their parents eat. If you sit down at the dinner table with a two-liter bottle of Coke, Jimmy won't ask for milk instead."[50]
>
> —Todd Zywicki, a professor at George Mason University School of Law.

Another common viewpoint is that what children and youth eat is ultimately the responsibility of parents. Although the marketing of fast food and other junk food may contribute to obesity, eating healthy is a learned behavior that starts in a child's home. Todd Zywicki is a law professor at George Mason University School of Law. He also served as the director of the Office of Policy Planning at the FTC from 2003 through 2004. Zywicki writes, "The underlying causes of weight gain in children are the same as in their parents—eating too much and exercising too little. And academic research confirms what we sense from personal experience: Kids eat what their parents eat. If you sit down at the dinner table with a two-liter bottle of Coke, Jimmy won't ask for milk instead."[50]

Moving Beyond Personal Responsibility

Critics of this view charge that society should not put all the onus on parents or the concept of personal responsibility because today's food culture—and the overzealous marketing that is part of it—make eating healthy extremely difficult. Even the most well-intentioned parents, some say, are no match for the marketing prowess of well-funded corporations that peddle hypersweetened beverages and highly palatable foods to kids. Health journalist and blogger Karen Cicero recalls how her young daughter got hooked on soda at a famed pizza restaurant known for its popular mouse mascot: "My daughter got her first taste of soda at a birthday party when she was 4. The lovely staff at Chuck E. Cheese's poured all the kids huge glasses of Sprite. Kate happily drank it all, claiming it was 'the best water ever' and then asked if we could get some for home. Thus, my battle over soda began."[51]

Although the marketing of fast food and other junk food may contribute to obesity, eating healthy is a learned behavior that starts in a child's home. Parents can help combat obesity in their children by modeling healthy eating habits and an active lifestyle.

For these reasons and more, many believe the country must move beyond the idea of personal responsibility and enact more stringent anti–junk food legislation at the federal level. Kelly Brownell is a Yale University professor of psychology and public health—and a vocal critic of the processed food industry. Brownell argues that government should regulate predatory junk food ads in the same way tobacco companies are regulated. Brownell says, "As a culture, we've become upset by the tobacco companies advertising to children, but we sit idly by while the food companies do the very same thing. And we could make a claim that the toll taken on the public health by a poor diet rivals that taken by tobacco."[52] When tobacco ads were restricted, smoking among youth declined dramatically. To many, however, this is an unfair comparison. As editorial writer Scott Faith states, "Fast food is no comparison to cigarettes. . . . While eating fast food in moderation will not cause severe long term effects, smoking just one cigarette can begin an addiction, which for some people will last a lifetime."[53]

A three-year research project called the Childhood Obesity Intervention Cost-Effectiveness Study (CHOICES) is attempting to assess the effectiveness of various proposed interventions that aim to reduce childhood obesity. CHOICES is a collaborative effort between the Harvard T.H. Chan School of Public Health, Columbia University's Mailman School of Public Health, and other research partners. Initial results suggest that eliminating the tax subsidy for advertising unhealthy foods and beverages on children's television is one of the most promising anti-obesity interventions. Under the current federal tax code, food companies can deduct expenses related to food advertising from their income taxes. Opponents wish to eliminate deductions if the advertising is for junk food. According to the CHOICES project, ending this tax loophole would give food companies an incentive to promote healthier options, which

> "As a culture, we've become upset by the tobacco companies advertising to children, but we sit idly by while the food companies do the very same thing."[52]
>
> —Kelly Brownell, a Yale University professor of psychology and public health.

could substantially lower BMI units in children. It would also generate $80 million a year and save close to $350 million in health care costs related to obesity and obesity-related diseases. This money, supporters say, could be earmarked for prevention efforts that could further reduce obesity.

Looking Ahead

Junk food marketing to children extends far beyond the country's borders; nations worldwide are grappling with these same issues. Although voluntary self-regulation remains the dominant strategy to restrict marketing of unhealthy foods, a number of countries are implementing legal strategies to address these forces that drive obesity. In 2006 the United Kingdom passed the world's first law restricting televised junk food advertising to children. The legislation placed restrictions on foods that contained high amounts of sugar, fat, and salt that were marketed to consumers younger than sixteen. By 2009 British children were exposed to 37 percent fewer junk food advertisements. In 2008 South Korea passed a similar law forbidding televised ads for junk food—primarily Western-made junk food that contained large amounts of sugar and fat—during children's prime viewing hours. Russia may soon follow: a member of parliament introduced a bill that would place restrictions on ads for sugary drinks, cookies, potato chips, and many other processed foods that appeal to children.

It Is too soon to tell whether this emerging tide of legislative action will succeed in lowering obesity rates. Whether the United States will follow suit and impose more stringent restrictions on food and drink industries will be wrestled out in the years to come.

Should Sugary Beverages Be Taxed?

Most public health experts agree that sugar has been a key player in the obesity epidemic. It is the most ubiquitous food ingredient in the world and is added to nearly all processed foods and drinks. Sugary drinks, in particular, are strongly associated with obesity and obesity-related health conditions, such as type 2 diabetes. Many health advocates believe a sugar tax would reduce the consumption of soda and other sweetened beverages, which has skyrocketed in recent decades.

The Birth of the Big Gulp

In a 7-Eleven store in California in 1976, the Big Gulp was born, beginning the era of supersized sodas weighing in at 32 ounces (1 L) or more. Before the Big Gulp, the average can of soda weighed 6 ounces (.2 L). Many health advocates believe it's no coincidence that obesity rates and consumption of these colossal drinks have risen in tandem. Today Americans drink, on average, 44 gallons (167 L) of soda per person, per year. In fact, soda is the most consumed drink in the United States; people drink almost twice as much soda as they do bottled water.

All this soda packs a sugary punch. A 12-ounce (.4 L) can of Coca-Cola weighs in with over nine teaspoons of sugar. Today's supersize versions pack a more powerful hit: a 42-ounce (1.2 L) size contains upwards of thirty teaspoons of added sugar. To put this in perspective, the American Heart Association recommends no more than six teaspoons of sugar per day for women or nine teaspoons for men. According to the Harvard T.H. Chan School of Public Health, however, more than 70 percent of Americans eat twenty-two teaspoons of added sugar every day. A 2011 UCB paper estimates that sweetened beverages account for almost half of these total added sugars in the American diet; in fact, soda contributes more sugar and calories to the diet than any other food or beverage.

Researchers report that these sugary drinks Americans are consuming add roughly 150 calories per day, which can lead to a

15-pound (7 kg) weight gain over the course of a year. Overweight consumers drink far more that that; over 10 percent of overweight adults drink more than 450 calories per day from sweetened beverages, or nearly three times the average consumed by adults.

"You Are What You Drink"

Barry Popkin is among the growing number of researchers who track the effects of diet on personal health. Popkin, who says "you are what you drink,"[54] believes all this sugar is having a harrowing effect on the nation's health and may be the single largest driver of rising obesity rates. According to Popkin and other health advocates, drinkable sugar is more troublesome than sweetened foods because sugared drinks don't lead to feelings of satiety, making it easy to consume too much. Children, moreover, may be particularly vulnerable to the ill health effects of soda. Research out of Harvard,

Before the 32-ounce Big Gulp was introduced by 7-Eleven in 1976, the average can of soda weighed just 6 ounces. Many health advocates believe it's no coincidence that obesity rates and the consumption of these colossal drinks have risen in tandem.

Sugary Foods and Drinks Are Not Addictive

J. Justin Wilson is the director of communications at the Institute for Justice. Here, Wilson makes the case for personal responsibility when it comes to sugar consumption.

When I was a kid, I dreaded trick-or-treating at my friend's house because I knew I was going to get a killjoy treat—specifically a toothbrush. I felt sorry for my friend even more: His mom told him he was "allergic" to sugar. . . .

Another horror story is that sugar is somehow addictive like cocaine. When researchers put people in a brain scanner and give them sugar, their brains' pleasure centers light up. But far from justifying the grim position of the toothbrush-and-celery brigades, this isn't significant.

Music causes similar reactions, but you don't hear people rushing to ban the Monster Mash. Any sort of enjoyment—whether eating candy, listening to music, playing video games, exercising, or falling in love—means that our brain's pleasure centers will light up, but not that the activity is drug-like.

Ultimately, solving the obesity problem is a matter of personal and parental responsibility.

J. Justin Wilson, "Concerns over Candy as an 'Addictive Drug' Are Overblown," Center for Consumer Freedom, October 28, 2012. www.consumerfreedom.com.

---

for example, shows that for each additional 12-ounce (.4 L) soda children consume per day, the risk of becoming obese increases by 60 percent.

Childhood obesity specialist Melinda Sothern relates the story of a morbidly obese child who was treated in her weight-loss clinic:

One 9-year-old girl who weighed over 300 pounds recently came to the clinic accompanied by her perplexed mother. The mom couldn't understand why her daughter was so large—after all, she didn't eat much. When questioned by the staff, the girl said she drank four or five 20-ounce [.6 L] sodas a day. That's about 1,000 to 1,250 calories a day. Another mystery solved. Of course, few children can stomach 100 ounces [3 L] of soda each day. . . . But plenty of kids manage to drink plenty of soda.[55]

Some People Find Sugary Soda Addictive

Ginger Christ is a newspaper reporter from Cleveland and a self-described former soda addict. She explains how her seeming dependence on soda once marked her daily routine.

It's been one year, five months and nearly one week since I've had a sip.

Of Mountain Dew.

Why did I stop? I think it was inevitable.

I'd quit in the past, usually for a week tops, because I could tell how dependent I was on Mountain Dew.

I would wake up in the morning and drink a can, or a bottle if it was a good day, at my desk. If I had to cover a meeting first thing, I'd pour Mountain Dew into a travel mug and position it next to my reporter's notebook. I carried a bottle in my purse . . . always.

The worst part probably was the effects I could feel on my body. Ignore my teeth, which obviously were impacted. . . . When I consumed too much, I could feel the sugar rushing through my veins. I used to joke I wanted a Mountain Dew IV, but, to be honest, I didn't need one. The absence of Mountain Dew could ruin a day, sending me into a groggy, irritated spiral. . . .

In the scheme of things, it's a small victory to quit drinking soda. . . . But, in the eyes of an addict, it's life changing.

Ginger Christ, "Confessions of a Recovering Mountain Dew Addict," Writer's Room, April 11, 2013. http://awritingcommunity.wordpress.com.

The Soda Ban

Stories like these have set off a global debate over how best to stem the flow of sugary drinks. In 2012 the mayor of New York City, Michael Bloomberg, proposed a ban on sodas over 16 ounces (.5 L) served at movie theaters, restaurants, and stadiums. Bloomberg called his Portion Cap Rule, commonly known as the Soda Ban, "the single biggest step any city . . . has taken to curb obesity."[56] The proposed ban generated nationwide controversy on the grounds that, if enacted, it would limit personal choice and lead to more intrusive government regulations. *USA Today* columnist Katrina Trinko is among those who believe that it should not be the role of government to influence what people eat or drink. As she says,

> Like most of us, I lived in an actual "nanny state" as a child, where my parents determined what I could eat and how much. Now, as an adult with the freedom to choose my own junk food consumption, I am overweight—which I wasn't as a kid. Nevertheless, irked as I am by my inability to commit to a healthier lifestyle, I wouldn't want to accept Bloomberg as my nanny. That's because I wouldn't trade a slimmer waist for being treated like a child again.[57]

Taxing Sugary Drinks

Although Bloomberg's ban was rejected in court, it put the issue of sugary drinks squarely before the public eye and informed the debate around other measures that target soda and other sugary drinks. Today a growing number of people support the imposition of taxes on sweetened beverages—and even other junk foods—to encourage people to choose healthier options. In addition to discouraging soda consumption, supporters say that money raised could offset health care costs and support public health and education programs, as tobacco taxes have done. Data from 1970 to 2007, for example, shows that raising cigarette prices through taxation led to lower usage. Roberta Friedman, director of public policy at the Rudd Center for Food Policy & Obesity, says, "[Tobacco taxes] reduced consumption considerably. . . . It worked beautifully. It's one of the major public health victories that we've had in the United States."[58]

Taxing drinks with added sugar is not a new idea. To date, thirty-four states have enacted a sales tax on sugary drinks. Sales tax, however, is paid at the checkout line, so consumers may not be aware they are paying extra for a sweetened beverage. For this reason, many tax supporters propose excise taxes—an indirect tax that raises the sticker price of a particular product—so that consumers can see that the price has gone up. If the ticket price of a soda goes up, the argument goes, consumers may think twice before purchasing it.

Excise Taxes

The proposal considered most often would introduce a penny-per-ounce excise tax on sodas and other sweetened drinks. Depending on the price of the product, this would raise the cost of the drink by about 15 to 20 percent, which, according to a handful of studies, would result in a 20 percent decrease in consumption. Some evidence suggests that this translates to weight reduction. A study by the Economic Research Service, an arm of the USDA, analyzed the effects of a hypothetical tax that induced a 20 percent increase in the retail price of sweetened beverages. Researchers estimate that this increase would reduce calorie intake from sweetened drinks by 13 percent for adults and 11 percent for children, which would translate into an average weight reduction of 3.8 pounds (1.7 kg) over a year for adults and 4.5 pounds (2 kg) for children.

While these outcomes appear promising, the idea of taxing sugar-sweetened beverages—or any food for that matter—has many critics. Jason Fletcher is a health economist at the University of Wisconsin. Fletcher's research suggests that soda taxes do little to combat obesity. Soda taxes, according to Fletcher, do correlate to slightly less soda consumption but not to a reduction in calories or weight because "people substitute other calories when they give up sodas."[59] William Shughart II, research director of the Independent Institute, also believes that the health benefits of a soda tax will be "vanishingly small." As he puts it, "Taxing sugary drinks does not reduce purchases enough to matter."[60] *Spectator* columnist Christopher Snowden puts forth more reasons why a soda tax might not work:

> Food is such a basic staple of the household budget that people either find ways to get around [taxes] or they simply pay up. Demand for tasty food is extremely inelastic. . . . No country has ever reduced obesity through taxation and the scale that would be required to make even a dent on obesity rates would be so vast that any government that attempted it would not be in government for very long.[61]

The Soda Industry Fights Back

The soda tax evokes a particularly intense outcry from the beverage industry, which insists that their products have been unfairly vilified in the obesity debate. According to the CSPI, soda companies have spent millions of dollars to advance this message. The group reports that since 2009, the soda industry has spent more than $106 million lobbying against antisoda initiatives.

Coca-Cola, the world's largest producer of sweetened drinks, has teamed up with a new nonprofit group called the Global Energy Balance Network. The group, which is funded by Coca-Cola, promotes the argument that soda is not the major culprit driving obesity. Steven Blair, vice president of the group, says, "Most of the focus in the popular media and in the scientific press is, 'Oh they're eating too much, eating too much, eating too much'—blaming fast food, blaming sugary drinks and so on. . . . And there's really virtually no compelling evidence that that, in fact, is the cause."[62] The scientists associated with the Global Energy Balance Network maintain that lack of physical activity, not the consumption of soda and other junk food, plays a larger role in today's swelling obesity rates.

"Food is such a basic staple of the household budget that people either find ways to get around [taxes] or they simply pay up."[61]

—*Spectator* columnist Christopher Snowden.

Sugar cubes are placed in front of a 64-ounce soda from Kentucky Fried Chicken. The cubes represent the total amount of sugar—217 grams—that is in the soda.

Those critical of the beverage industry claim that statements like these are part of a larger effort to deflect attention away from anti–sugary drink initiatives. Today a number of cities and states are forging ahead to circumvent the beverage industry and other opponents of soda taxation. To date, few lawmakers have succeeded in passing a sugar tax, but that dynamic may be changing. Public health officials hope that empirical data coming in from Mexico, which recently approved a countrywide tax on sweetened beverages, will provide some insight.

The Mexican Soda Tax

Mexico's antiobesity program has attracted worldwide attention. Roughly 70 percent of the population is overweight or obese, and close to 12 percent of the adult population has type 2 diabetes. Many public health advocates believe soda may be partly to blame for these discouraging trends: Mexicans are the largest consumers of soda in the world; soda intake accounts for fully 70 percent of the added sugar consumed by the average citizen. As part of a broader program to attack these trends, Mexico, in 2013, passed a one-peso-per-liter tax on sugary drinks, which raised their prices by 10 percent. The tax is nationwide.

To assess whether the tax had any impact on soda consumption, a team of researchers from Mexico's federal public health agency, the Instituto Nacional de Salud Pública, and the University of North Carolina at Chapel Hill compared soda sales before and after the tax took effect. After one year, the tax appeared to be working: the sale of sugary beverages decreased roughly 12 percent, and bottled water purchases rose 4 percent. As Juan Rivera, one of the study's authors, says, "In the area of obesity prevention and control, there are not many examples of measures that actually work . . . but these findings suggest that the tax is working and that it's reducing the intake of sugar sweetened beverages. This is really important for Mexico and the world."[63]

At the same time, a report out of the Mexico Institute of Technology, funded by ConMexico, an industry trade group that includes Coca-Cola, Pepsi, and other large drink companies, suggests that Mexico's soda tax, even if it has a minimal effect on how much soda Mexicans are drinking, will not have any meaningful impact on the country's soaring obesity rates. Other reports suggest the tax is not widely popular. Data from polls conducted by the Toronto-based research company RIWI in August 2015 found that "the majority of total respondents (62%) do not support higher taxes as a way to reduce obesity in Mexico."[64] Only 44 percent of those polled, moreover, even knew about the tax implemented the year before.

> "[The Mexican soda tax] is working and . . . it's reducing the intake of sugar sweetened beverages."[63]
>
> —Juan Rivera, a professor of nutrition in the Instituto Nacional de Salud Pública.

Opponents also contend that soda taxes are regressive, meaning they disproportionately fall on individuals with the lowest income—that is, people who can afford them the least. Some observers, however, say that this might not be such a bad thing, as obesity and diabetes disproportionately affect lower-income populations, which tend to drink more soda. As Kelly Brownell puts it,

Critics . . . argue that taxes on sugary beverages are regressive and would hurt the poor, but obesity and diabetes are highly regressive diseases. Tobacco taxes helped prevent cancer and heart disease among those least able to afford the medical care these diseases require. Furthermore, the revenue from soda taxes could be used to help those most in need by subsidizing the costs of foods like fruits and vegetables.[65]

Whether decreased soda consumption in Mexico will translate into lower obesity rates will be determined as more data is gathered in the years ahead. In the meantime, legislators on the other side of the border are testing the waters to ascertain whether similar measures will improve public health.

Other Taxation Experiments

In the fall of 2014, Berkeley, California, became the first city in the United States to approve a penny-per-ounce tax on sugared drinks, despite the soda industry's $2.5 million campaign opposing the tax.

In an effort to slow climbing obesity rates, some states have imposed a special tax on foods with little nutritional value, such as sweetened beverages, cookies, and chips. The tax money collected is then used to fund valuable health-promoting programs.

As Berkeley mayor Tom Bates said at the time, "We're saying no to Big Soda. . . . We're saying that Berkeley and the rest of the country need to pay attention that soda is such a destructive product."[66] Although it is too early to tell if Berkeley's soda tax is turning consumers away from soda or putting a dent in obesity rates, the tax generated $100,000 in revenue during its first month. These funds, supporters say, are being used to support valuable health-promoting programs.

A similar taxation experiment is under way in parts of New Mexico, Utah, and Arizona, in a region that is home to the Navajo Nation, a community with high rates of obesity and diabetes. Unlike taxes in Mexico and Berkeley, the Navajo Nation voted in November 2014 to impose a 2 percent tax on a broad array of foods with little nutritional value. Foods that qualify for the tax include sweetened beverages, cookies, chips, and other snacks—the types of highly processed and highly caloric foods that are abundantly available in the Navajo Nation. Many residents fear the tax is doomed to failure, however, because access to fruits, vegetables, and other healthy foods is extremely limited in this area. As one tribal member explains, "You can tax them as much as you want but they will still buy [junk food] because that's the only thing that is available."[67] Tribal leaders hope that tax revenues, slated at $1 million a year, will be used not only to discourage junk food consumption but also to encourage people to grow gardens, raise livestock, and open farmers' markets. For now, it is too soon to tell whether these efforts will change the group's food buying habits—and curb the obesity rates that are almost three times the national average.

The movement to slash obesity rates via a sugar tax picked up some steam in March 2015, when federal legislatures introduced the Sugar-Sweetened Beverage Tax Act of 2015, a bill more commonly known as the SWEET Act. If passed, this legislation would levy an excise tax of one penny per teaspoon of caloric sweetener. Supporters say that at the very least, measures like these will make people more aware of the link between heavy sugar consumption and obesity, diabetes, and other chronic health problems. Whether the SWEET Act and other antisugar initiatives will halt rising rates of obesity will be seen in the years ahead.

Introduction: A Global Phenomenon

1. Harriet Brown, "The Weight of the Evidence," *Slate,* March 24, 2015. www.slate.com.
2. Christopher J.L. Murray, "Nearly One-third of the World's Population Is Obese or Overweight, New Data Show," Institute for Health Metrics and Evaluation, 2016. www.healthdata.org.
3. Harvard T.H. Chan School of Public Health, "Obesity Prevention Strategies," 2016. www.hsph.harvard.edu.

Chapter 1: What Are the Facts?

4. World Health Organization, "Obesity and Overweight," January 2015. www.who.int.
5. *UC Berkeley Wellness Letter,* "The Girth of a Nation," Fall 2015, p. 1. www.berkeleywellness.com.
6. Quoted in Pam Belluck, "Children's Life Expectancy Being Cut Short by Obesity," *New York Times,* March 17, 2005. www.nytimes.com.
7. Jamie Lee Peterson, "From the Schoolyard to Your Yard: Cyber-Bullying Brings Victimization Home," Obesity Action Coalition, 2016. www.obesityaction.org.
8. Christine R. Brass, "Experiences of an Obese Patient," *Narrative Inquiry in Bioethics*, vol. 4, no. 2, Summer 2014. http://muse.jhu.edu.
9. Anonymous One, "My Story: Evolving Obesities," *Narrative Inquiry in Bioethics*, vol. 4, no. 2, Summer 2014. http://muse.jhu.edu.
10. Quoted in Mission: Readiness, *Too Fat to Fight: Retired Military Leaders Want Junk Food Out of America's Schools,* 2010. www.missionreadiness.org.
11. Quoted in Trust for America's Health, *F as in Fat: How Obesity Threatens America's Future 2013,* August 2013, p. 27. http://healthyamericans.org.

Chapter 2: Should Government Regulate Access to Junk Food?

12. Christina Roberto, "Patchy Progress on Obesity Prevention: Emerging Examples, Entrenched Barriers, and New Thinking," *Lancet*, February 18, 2015. www.thelancet.com.

13. Deborah A. Cohen, *A Big Fat Crisis: The Hidden Forces Behind the Obesity Epidemic—and How We Can End It.* New York: Nation, 2014, p. 8.
14. Janet Currie et al., "The Effects of Fast Food Restaurants on Obesity," National Bureau of Economic Research, December 5, 2011. www.nber.org.
15. Quoted in Alicia Chang, "Study: Fast-food Limits Didn't Cut Obesity Rate in South LA," *JDNews,* March 23, 2015. www.jdnews.com.
16. Jennifer M. Poti, Kiyah J. Duffey, and Barry M. Popkin, "The Association of Fast Food Consumption with Poor Dietary Outcomes and Obesity Among Children: Is It the Fast Food or the Remainder of Diet?," *American Journal of Clinical Nutrition*, October 23, 2013. http://ajcn.nutrition.org.
17. David R. Just and Brian Wansink, "Fast Food, Soft Drink, and Candy Intake Is Unrelated to Body Mass Index for 95% of American Adults," *Obesity Science & Practice*, 2015. http://onlinelibrary.wiley.com.
18. Quoted in CBS, "Study: Zoning Law Limiting Fast-Food Outlets Did Not Cut Obesity Rate in South LA," March 18, 2015. http://losangeles.cbslocal.com.
19. Quoted in Tara Haelle, "Research: Childhood Obesity Is a Product of Environment," *Salon*, April 9, 2013. www.salon.com.
20. Quoted in USDA, "Obama Administration Details Healthy Food Financing Intitiative," news release, February 9, 2010. www.usda.gov.
21. Quoted in Patrick Rogers, "Building Healthier Communities with Homegrown Foodies," Next City, October 23, 2015. http://nextcity.org.
22. Cohen, *A Big Fat Crisis*, p. 80.
23. Quoted in Christian Nordqvist, "No Single Approach Will Solve America's Obesity Epidemic," *Medical News Today*, July 14, 2011. www.medicalnewstoday.com.
24. David R. Just and Brian Wansink, "School Nutrition: A Kid's Right to Choose," *Los Angeles Times,* February 3, 2012. www.latimes.com.
25. Just and Wansink, "School Nutrition."

Chapter 3: Can Educational Programs Help Control Obesity?

26. David A. Kessler, *The End of Overeating: Taking Control of the Insatiable American Appetite*. New York: Rodale, 2009, p. 249.
27. Michael F. Jacobson, "Ending Food Ignorance: Education Is Too Important to Leave to Big Food," Huffington Post, September 7, 2013. www.huffingtonpost.com.
28. Let's Move!, "Learn the Facts," 2010. www.letsmove.gov.
29. Quoted in Krissah Thompson, "Michelle Obama Keeps Moving with 'Let's Move,'" *Washington Post,* February 9, 2012. www.washingtonpost.com.
30. Quoted in Darlene Superville, "Michelle Obama Says 'Let's Move!' Program Is 'Changing the Conversation,'" Huffington Post, September 9, 2013. www.huffingtonpost.com.
31. Robert H. Lustig, *Fat Chance: Beating the Odds Against Sugar, Processed Food, Obesity, and Disease.* New York: Penguin, 2012, p. 259.
32. Quoted in Becky Bach, "Lack of Exercise, Not Diet, Linked to Rise in Obesity, Stanford Research Shows," Stanford Medicine News Center, July 2014. http://med.stanford.edu.
33. Chris Woolston, "Why Is There an Obesity Epidemic?," HealthDay, January 20, 2016. www.healthday.com.
34. Let's Move!, "Get Active," 2010. www.letsmove.gov.
35. Jayne Hurley and Bonnie Liebman, "The 9 Worst Chain Restaurant Meals of the Year," *Nutrition Action Health Letter*, June 2015. www.cspinet.org.
36. Center for Science in the Public Interest, "Menu Labeling," 2016. www.cspinet.org.
37. Quoted in Liz Thatcher, "New Study Proves Menu Labeling Doesn't Work as Promised," *Washington Examiner,* August 6, 2013. www.washingtonexaminer.com.
38. Joanne E. Arsenault, "Can Nutrition Labeling Affect Obesity?," *Choices,* 2010. www.choicesmagazine.org.

Chapter 4: Should the Marketing of Food to Children Be Restricted?

39. Kellogg Company, *2008 Annual Report*. www.slideshare.net.
40. Jacobson, "Ending Food Ignorance."

41. Committee on Food Marketing and the Diets of Children and Youth, *Food Marketing to Children and Youth: Threat or Opportunity*. Washington, DC: National Academies, December 5, 2005. www.nationalacademies.org.
42. Better Business Bureau, "Children's Food and Beverage Advertising Initiative," 2016. www.bbb.org.
43. Better Business Bureau, "Progress Continues in Food Advertising Self-Regulation Program," December 19, 2012. www.bbb.org.
44. Campaign for a Commercial-Free Childhood, "Food Marketing and Childhood Obesity," 2016. www.commercialfreechildhood.org.
45. Quoted in Alexandra Sifferlin, "How to Choose a Healthy Breakfast Cereal," CNN, July 6, 2012. www.cnn.com.
46. Lustig, *Fat Chance,* p. 17.
47. Center for Consumer Freedom, "What Is the Center for Consumer Freedom?," 2015. www.consumerfreedom.com.
48. Center for Consumer Freedom, "Food Marketing Bans Take a Beating," April 13, 2012. www.consumerfreedom.com.
49. Susan Linn and Michele Simon, "The Dark Side of Marketing Healthy Food to Children," Huffington Post, August 19, 2013. www.huffingtonpost.com.
50. Todd Zywicki, "SpongeBob SquarePants' Last Stand," *Wall Street Journal*, April 12, 2012. www.wsj.com.
51. Karen Cicero, "Do Your Kids Drink Too Much Soda?," Pediatric Safety, January 11, 2013. www.pediatricsafety.net.
52. Quoted in Michael Moss, "The Extraordinary Science of Addictive Junk Food," *New York Times*, February 20, 2013. www.nytimes.com.
53. Scott Faith, "The Government and My Waistline," *Havok Journal*, September 30, 2014. http://havokjournal.com.

Chapter 5: Should Sugary Beverages Be Taxed?

54. Quoted in Susan Shackelford, "No Sugar-Coating the Crusade Against Obesity," *Carolina Public Health*, Spring 2010. http://sph.unc.edu.
55. Quoted in Chris Woolston, "At a Time When More Kids Are Overweight and Obese than Ever, Why Are Soft Drinks More Popular than Ever?," HealthDay, January 20, 2016. www.healthday.com.

56. Quoted in Michael M. Grynbaum, "Health Panel Approves Restriction on Sale of Large Sugary Drinks," *New York Times*, September 13, 2012. www.nytimes.com.

57. Katrina Trinko, "Soda Ban? What About Personal Choice?," *USA Today*, March 10, 2013. www.usatoday.com.

58. Quoted in Elizabeth Whitman, "A Turning Point for Soda Taxes? In Illinois, Big Soda May Not Win Battle Against Levies on Sugary Drinks," *International Business Times*, September 3, 2015. www.ibtimes.com.

59. Quoted in Karen Faster, "Research Finds Soda Tax Does Little to Decrease Obesity," *University of Wisconsin, Madison, News*, March 24, 2014. http://news.wisc.edu.

60. William Shughart II, "NO: The Health Benefits Are Far Less Than Claimed," in *Wall Street Journal*, "Should There Be a Tax on Soda and Other Sugary Drinks?," July 12, 2015. www.wsj.com.

61. Christopher Snowden, "A Tax on Sugar Won't Work, as the Shipwreck of the Danish 'Fat Tax' Shows," *Spectator Health* (blog), May 22, 2015. http://blogs.spectator.co.uk.

62. Quoted in Anahad O'Connor, "Coca-Cola Funds Scientists Who Shift Blame for Obesity away from Bad Diets," *New York Times*, August 9, 2015. www.nytimes.com.

63. Quoted in Anahad O'Connor, "Mexican Soda Tax Followed by Drop in Sugary Drink Sales," *New York Times*, January 6, 2016. www.newyorktimes.com.

64. RIWI, "Mexico Beverage Tax Study," 2015. http://riwi.com.

65. Kelly Brownell, "YES: It Is an Effective Way to Cut Obesity and the Harm It Does," in *Wall Street Journal*, "Should There Be a Tax on Soda and Other Sugary Drinks?," July 12, 2015. www.wsj.com.

66. Quoted in Rong-Gong Lin II, "Tax on Sugary Drinks Approved in Berkeley; S.F. Measure Falls Short," *Los Angeles Times*, November 5, 2014. www.latimes.com.

67. Quoted in Elizabeth Whitman, "Navajo Reservation Taxes Junk Food but Provides Few Fresh Food Alternatives for Community with High Rates of Diabetes and Obesity," *International Business Times*, April 9, 2015. www.ibtimes.com.

Center for Science in the Public Interest (CSPI)
1220 L. St. NW, Suite 300
Washington, DC 20005
phone: (202) 332-9110

The CSPI is a nonprofit organization that promotes awareness about nutrition, food safety, alcohol, the environment, and other health issues. The CSPI's award-winning newsletter, *Nutrition Action Healthletter,* is the largest circulating newsletter in North America.

Centers for Disease Control and Prevention (CDC)
1600 Clifton Rd.
Atlanta, GA 30329
phone: (800) 232-4636
website: www.cdc.gov

The CDC is part of the US Department of Health and Human Services. The CDC works to maintain the health of the nation's citizens and prevent chronic diseases. Part of the CDC's website is devoted to nutrition, physical activity, and the prevention of obesity.

National Association for the Advancement of Fat Acceptance (NAAFA)
website: www.naafaonline.com

NAAFA is a civil rights organization devoted to eliminating discrimination based on body size and protecting the rights of people whom society labels as fat or obese. NAAFA strives to end fat bias in the health care system, the educational system, and the workplace.

National Childhood Obesity Foundation (NCOF)
40 South St., Suite 304
Marblehead, MA 01945
phone: (781) 639-0048
website: www.ncof.org

The NCOF seeks to reduce the debilitating effects of childhood obesity. To this end, it strives to serve as a global leader in nutrition and physical activity education for parents, teachers, health care professionals, and others who care for children.

Obesity Action Coalition (OAC)

4511 N. Himes Ave., Suite 250
Tampa, FL 33614
phone: (800) 717-3117
website: www.obesityaction.org

The OAC is a nonprofit organization dedicated to improving the lives of those affected by obesity through education, support, and advocacy. The OAC seeks to raise awareness about obesity and improve access to treatment and prevention.

Obesity Society

8757 Georgia Ave., Suite 1320
Silver Spring, MD 20910
phone: (301) 563-6595
website: www.obesity.org

The Obesity Society is a nonprofit scientific and educational organization that seeks to advance the understanding of the causes, consequences, prevention, and treatment of obesity. The society publishes two journals, *Obesity* and *Obesity Science & Practice.*

Rudd Center for Food Policy & Obesity

University of Connecticut
1 Constitution Plaza, Suite 600
Hartford, CT 06103
phone: (860) 380-1000
website: www.uconnruddcenter.org

The Rudd Center for Food Policy & Obesity is a nonprofit organization that strives to end childhood obesity, poor diet, and weight bias. To this end, the Rudd Center conducts research to inform public policy and advocacy and supports evidence-based solutions to the obesity problem.

Books

Anna Bellisari, *The Anthropology of Obesity in the United States*. New York: Routledge, 2016.

Anna Bellisari, *The Obesity Epidemic in North America: Connecting Biology and Culture.* Longrove, IL: Waveland, 2013.

Laura Dawes, *Childhood Obesity in America: Biography of an Epidemic*. Cambridge, MA: Harvard University Press, 2014.

Michael Moss, *Salt Sugar Fat: How the Food Giants Hooked Us*. New York: Random House, 2013.

Marion Nestle and Malden Nesheim, *Why Calories Count: From Science to Politics*. Berkeley and Los Angeles: University of California Press, 2012.

Michael J. Power and Jay Schulkin, *The Evolution of Obesity*. Baltimore: Johns Hopkins University Press, 2009.

Mark Schatzker, *The Dorito Effect: The Surprising New Truth About Food and Flavor.* New York: Simon & Schuster, 2015.

Jacob Warren and K. Bryant Smalley, *Always the Fat Kid: The Truth About the Enduring Effects of Childhood Obesity.* London: Palgrave Macmillan, 2013.

Internet Sources

Prevention Institute, "The Facts on Junk Food Marketing and Kids," 2015. www.preventioninstitute.org/focus-areas/supporting -healthy-food-a-activity/supporting-healthy-food-and-activity -environments-advocacy/get-involved-were-not-buying-it/735 -were-not-buying-it-the-facts-on-junk-food-marketing-and-kids|. html.

Trust for America's Health, *F as in Fat: How Obesity Threatens America's Future 2013,* August 2013. http://healthyamericans .org/report/108.

Trust for America's Health, *The State of Obesity 2015,* September 2015. http://healthyamericans.org/reports/stateofobesity2015.

Ellen Wartella, "Food Marketing and Childhood Obesity," Northwestern University, January 30, 2015. http://discover.northwestern.edu/stories/food-marketing-and-childhood-obesity.

Websites

Harvard T.H. Chan School of Public Health Obesity Prevention Source (www.hsph.harvard.edu). The Obesity Prevention Source, part of the Department of Nutrition at Harvard School of Public Health, is an in-depth resource that provides science-based information about the causes, consequences, prevention, and control of obesity.

Let's Move! (www.letsmove.gov). This program, developed by First Lady Michelle Obama, seeks to solve the problem of childhood obesity by providing schools, families, and communities with resources to help kids develop healthy lifestyles.

Robert Wood Johnson Foundation, Childhood Obesity (www.rwjf.org). This foundation supports scientific research, changes to community environments, and public policy initiatives that address America's childhood obesity epidemic.

Shape Up America (http://shapeup.org). This national program seeks to promote awareness about the health risks related to obesity and to provide information on healthy weight management for all.

INDEX

Note: Boldface page numbers indicate illustrations.